GOAT WORLD

HOW TO AVOID POPULATION COLLAPSE, ESCAPE WORLDWIDE UNEMPLOYMENT, AND BUILD A FUTURE OF LIFE, LOVE, AND WEALTH FOR ALL HUMANITY

GOAT WORLD

HOW TO AVOID POPULATION COLLAPSE, ESCAPE WORLDWIDE UNEMPLOYMENT, AND BUILD A FUTURE OF LIFE, LOVE, AND WEALTH FOR ALL HUMANITY

PAUL J. EBREO

Printed in the United States of America

Published by Abundance Collective
PO Box 43, Powell, OH 43065

LCCN: 2025912708
Paperback ISBN: 978-1-965419-18-2
Hardcover ISBN: 978-1-965419-19-9
e-book ISBN: 978-1-965419-20-5

Available in paperback, hardcover, e-book, and audiobook.

First edition published 2024
Paperback ISBN: 978-1-965419-00-7
Hardback ISBN: 978-1-965419-01-4
eBook ISBN: 978-1-965419-02-1

To Mama, you made me the person who I am.
I love you forever and ever.
—PJ

TABLE OF CONTENTS

Part 1: Setting the Pieces

Part 2: Playing Our Cards Right

Part 3: End Game

When there is scarcity, the worst of humans come out.
When abundance for all, the best in all.
—Paul J. Ebreo

PART 1

Setting the Pieces

And if I have the gift of prophecy and comprehend all mysteries and all knowledge; if I have all faith so as to move mountains but do not have love, I am nothing.
—1 Corinthians 13:2 (New American Bible)

If I have seen further, it is because I have stood on the shoulders of giants.
—Isaac Newton

Deshi Basara (Rise)

In a dusty field, picked clean by countless hooves, lived a goat named Joaquin. The grass was brown, and the air stale. A deep discontent gnawed at him. One night, Joaquin dreamt of a lush green valley where goats frolicked and the grass shimmered like emeralds. Waking with a start, he knew he had to find this paradise.

Legend spoke of a bridge leading to such a land, nestled high in the mountains. Determined, Joaquin began his climb. The way was treacherous, with rocky slopes giving way to sheer cliffs. He narrowly escaped from mountain lions and dodged falling stones. Other goats, content in their familiar dust, bleated taunts ...

Preamble

Maya clutched the worn handlebars of the rickety roller coaster, heart hammering a frantic rhythm against her ribs. Below, the twisted metal track snaked through the park, a steel serpent promising both terror and exhilaration. Her best friend, Kai, beside her, sported a wide, confident grin.

"Ready to dissect the G-forces later, science girl?" he teased.

Maya rolled her eyes. "Always. But that doesn't mean I can't enjoy the ride, does it?"

Their high school physics class had recently delved into gravity, its formulas and calculations etched into Maya's mind. Yet, the intellectual understanding couldn't diminish the primal fear bubbling in her stomach as the coaster lurched forward. The first climb, agonizingly slow, stretched out the anticipation. Then, the crest.

The world tilted on its axis. The wind roared, whipping through Maya's hair as they plummeted down the first drop. Her stomach lurched with a freefall sensation that defied logic. But amidst the terror, a strange sense of awe blossomed. It was like peering behind the curtain of reality, witnessing the invisible force that held them to the earth yet flung them weightless through the air.

Each twist and turn was a testament to physics in action. The loops, inverting their vision, were a demonstration of centripetal force. The tight corners, pinning them to their seats, showcased the effects of inertia. Yet, the science only amplified the experience. It wasn't a sterile equation on a whiteboard; it was a living, breathing force orchestrating their wild ride.

As the coaster finally screeched to a halt, Maya emerged, legs wobbling, a wide grin splitting her face.

Kai, a bit pale but still chuckling, nudged her. "So, anything new to report, Professor Gravity?"

Maya laughed. "Just that the thrill is all the sweeter when you understand the magic behind it." They walked away, legs shaky but spirits soaring, a testament to the fact that science could illuminate the wonders of the world, not steal from them. The roller coaster ride, a symphony of physics, would forever be etched in Maya's memory, a thrilling blend of science and pure, unadulterated fun.

Unveiling the Mystery Doesn't Spoil the Magic

There is a fear, unjustified or not, that scientific understanding diminishes the richness of experience. Demystifying the world, the thinking goes, removes the wonder.

On the other hand, an intellectual understanding of gravity—its force, its pull—doesn't diminish the visceral thrill of the ride. In fact, it might even add to it. Now, both your emotions and intellect are stimulated.

Take the realm of consciousness itself. Does understanding the intricate networks of neurons firing in our brains diminish the mystery of human experience? Does it lessen the awe we feel gazing at a starry night sky or the heart-wrenching emotions evoked by a powerful piece of music?

What if I explain, without pretense or mysticism, what intelligence is and how to build synthetic intelligence? With this understanding we could solve humanity's biggest problems. We could revolutionize fields like medicine, energy, and space exploration. The possibilities are nearly endless.

TLDR: An explanation of why and how things work doesn't diminish the experience of that being explained. It might even enhance it.

The Plan

Our world today faces serious challenges: war, poverty, hunger, population collapse, and the growing fear of artificial intelligence.

These are gigantic issues, but there are also a lot of exciting new technologies developing right now in front of us, ready to solve them and unlock an incredible new way forward. This book describes an ambitious plan to harness them and upgrade humanity. Here it is in a nutshell.

First and foremost, we must adopt an antifragile mindset. Let's embrace life's inevitable messiness and turbulence and use it to grow. Think of a hydra: cut off a head, and two more grow.

Next, we harness the power of human-level intelligence and beyond. To do that, we must first redefine intelligence and pinpoint our understanding of consciousness. Then, we apply an AI architecture that is human-aligned and completely explainable, understandable, and affordable to all. Only by fulfilling these requirements can we be ready to engineer AI and robots that are at least as capable as humans.

To address population collapse, we need a two-part solution. First, let's reimagine love. Maybe traditional models don't quite fit everyone. Let's destigmatize exploring different relationship structures, like ethical non-monogamy (ENM). Also, let's re-emphasize the core of relationships: honesty, communication, and vulnerability.

Next is the second part of the solution and the next game-changer: karma socioeconomics. Imagine a system built on human-aligned AI and blockchain. The AI is transparent and works for everyone, not just a privileged few. Blockchain keeps things secure, and everyone's on the same page. It sounds ambitious, but with the convergence of technology, it's within humanity's grasp.

The result? A world where hunger, poverty, and disease become relics of the past. War? It becomes a painful, distant memory.

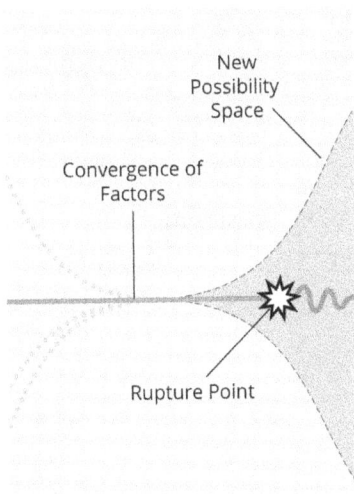

RethinkX presents the idea of a convergence of factors that opens up a system to new possibilities.[1] We can then apply the meeting of incredible new technologies to upgrade our social and economic systems. While the series of factors I present come from varying disciplines, the convergence of these factors opens up an almost unbelievable new future for humanity.

Infinite growth will be possible and even encouraged. Human connection will thrive, and innovation will explode as every person becomes an Innovator. This would be a whole new era for humanity: one built on the power of diverse experiences and a **drive** to explore the unknown. Now, that's a future worth getting excited about. That's the future I present to you here, but it all starts with setting the pieces on the board. We start first with upgrading our mindsets…

Why This Would Work

- The technologies to facilitate the plan are built and set up.
- We have seen the successful convergence of technologies before.[2]
- More people see the need for the upgrade every day.

What Will Happen

- Breath-taking possibilities will unfold before our eyes.
- Infinite growth for humanity will be possible in any realm you can imagine.

The Road to Antifragility

His eyes open. Just for a few moments as he falls back to sleep to the sound of the ventilator.

Within three months, Roderigo's world had shrunk faster than a line of compiled code. First, his mom. A quiet thief, cancer had stolen her strength, then her smile, and finally, her life. Then, the world outside his window followed suit. A triple whammy: his beloved mother's death, a global pandemic, and a massive stroke. There were no visitors allowed during the initial outbreak.

He, a programmer, naturally liked being alone, but this situation pushed that limit. His hospital room was sterile and quiet; his only companions were the tubes sticking out of his body, the beeps of machines, and the nurses' gentle but fleeting moments of small talk.

But changing from his computer screen-lit existence wouldn't be a simple reboot. The outside world, once a blur of deadlines and takeout containers, now seemed as alien as a foreign language. How could he, a man who navigated virtual worlds with ease, struggle to hold a spoon?

It would be far from a simple reboot. He had to re-learn how to stand, walk, and even swallow water again. He started small, regaining control over his fingers with repetitive exercises that felt more like debugging stubborn code. Each regained movement was a compiled line, a step closer to a functional him. He devoured physical therapy sessions, the once-agonizing stretches becoming a challenge to be conquered.

The forced isolation wasn't all bad. Time, once a luxury programmer life rarely afforded, stretched before him, his thoughts a vast unexplored territory. His body, betrayed by the stroke, became a constant reminder of another truth, a truth so obvious it was easy to overlook: health was the ultimate wealth.

He vowed to change his lifestyle completely.

TLDR: Without health, material comforts mean very little.

The Antifragile Mindset

The concept of antifragility, popularized by author Nassim Taleb in his book *Antifragile,* describes the true opposite of fragility. It goes beyond the ability to withstand difficulty; instead, it **gains** from it. Someone who is truly antifragile uses difficulty to thrive.

Fragile   Resilient   Antifragile

Taleb uses three metaphors from Greek mythology to explain the concept. Damocles, a figure with a sword perpetually hanging over his head, represents constant threat and vulnerability. The Phoenix that rises from the ashes embodies resilience and the ability to bounce back from destruction. Finally, the Hydra, a many-headed serpent where cutting off one head leads to two growing back, represents antifragility. In other words, antifragility is not just resilience. Rather, it's about thriving on stressors, growing stronger, and feeding on challenges.[3]

These three images capture the essence of fragility, resilience, and antifragility.

Bodybuilding exemplifies antifragility beautifully. Each grueling workout, each set pushed to failure, is a micro-trauma. Muscles tear, the body screams, and you want to quit. But within this discomfort lies the potential for growth.

Think of it like this: when a weightlifter progressively increases the load on their muscles, they're not just building bigger muscles. They're forcing their bodies to adapt. Bones become denser, tendons and ligaments strengthen, and the nervous system fine-tunes movement patterns. This adaptation isn't just about aesthetics; it's about building a body that's more robust, more resistant to future injuries, and capable of handling even greater challenges.

Why does stress (to a certain point) spur muscle growth? The answer is hormesis, which is a biological phenomenon where exposure to a low dose of a stressor or toxin can benefit an organism. It's essentially the idea that a little bit of stress can be good for you because your body naturally overcompensates so that it will be ready for next time.

Similarly, embracing an antifragile mindset helps build mental strength. It can be a metaphor for life's journey. With this mindset, you can face the discomfort of the unknown, venture outside your comfort zone, and explore new possibilities and opportunities.

August

August sprinted through the park, lungs burning but a smile splitting her face. Her mental health therapist had encouraged her to find a physical outlet for her stress. But here she was, chasing pigeons (mostly winning) and feeling a lightness she hadn't experienced in weeks.

It all started with a promotion. A bigger paycheck, yes; new teammates to worry about, certainly; and more responsibility, definitely. Yet, August had felt like a deflated balloon. Sleep evaded her, replaced by a constant low-grade anxiety. Workdays bled into nights and the vibrant artist she once was had become a ghost, replaced by a productivity machine.

For August, therapy sessions were still crucial, a space to untangle the knots of anxiety and self-doubt. At the same time, exercise definitely helped. So the park became her sanctuary, a place where the chatter in her mind quieted, and a new kind of strength emerged.

There, she reset both her mind and body. For her, it was also a reminder that mental and physical health weren't separate entities but rather two sides of the same well-being coin. And that, August realized with a grin as she chased another unsuspecting pigeon, was a truth worth celebrating.

TLDR: Both physical and mental health should be paid attention to and taken care of.

Antifragile Entrepreurship

The worlds of business and philosophy might seem like strange bedfellows, but a closer look reveals a fascinating parallel: antifragility and lean startups. Both celebrate the power of the unexpected—the notion that undesirable or unpredictable situations can actually lead to growth and success.

For the antifragile system, negative occurrences aren't just tolerated; they're actively beneficial. I've presented that the antifragile system thrives on challenges and setbacks. Similarly, imagine a business that uses customer complaints to refine its product or service, emerging from the experience stronger and more adaptable.

A key difference is that the core tenet of lean startups embraces methodical experimentation, rapid iteration, and continuous refinements. Lean startups don't wait for a perfectly polished product before hitting the market. Instead, they launch minimum viable products (MVPs), gather real-world user data, and adapt their offerings based on the sometimes unpredictable results.

Both antifragility and lean startups challenge the traditional risk-averse approach to success. They remind us that the path to progress is rarely linear and that sometimes the greatest opportunities lie hidden within the unexpected.

By turning adversity into advantage and embracing the unknown, both philosophies unlock the way to incredible new heights.

Danny

Danny "Fingers" Fontana, once a trumpet player known for his lightning-fast runs and smoky speakeasy gigs, was facing his own financial blues. His restaurant, "The Blues Burger Joint," hemorrhaged cash. The rent, overdue for the third month in a row, loomed as large as a grand piano.

Danny, at 58, wasn't built for spreadsheets. He thrived on improvisation, not financial projections. But staring at the eviction notice, improvisation wouldn't pay the bills. He needed a new melody, a business riff. He remembered his granddaughter, Charlotte, a tech whiz studying something called "Lean Startups." The basic idea was to learn through a systematic approach of trial and error. As a musician used to practice, it made total sense.

Over steaming mugs of chamomile tea (Danny couldn't stomach coffee anymore), Charlotte explained. "Forget the big plans, Grandpa. Let's test things out in small batches, like you do with your trumpet solos. Using small failures to create big wins. You know, like when you learn how to play a new tune." The light bulb flickered on above Danny's head. He wouldn't chase a single, risky venture. He'd play multiple smaller tunes and see which tunes the audience (customers) liked or didn't like.

Their first gig (experiment)? A pop-up jazz bar in a nearby park. Danny dusted off his trumpet, its sheen dulled from disuse. Charlotte, with her infectious enthusiasm, whipped up social media buzz. The park, bathed in the golden glow of the setting sun, became an impromptu concert hall. Danny's fingers, surprisingly nimble, coaxed life back into the old horn. The crowd, a mix of curious teenagers and nostalgic retirees, swayed to the music. The hat Danny held at the end overflowed with bills, not coins. Not a fortune, but enough for him to buy groceries and feel a spark of hope.

Next, he and Charlotte refreshed the restaurant's menu. They ditched the generic burger options and went all in on Danny's own history. The menu became a musical odyssey, a tribute to the greats he played alongside. The "Dizzy Gillespie" featured a dizzying array of toppings – kimchi, pickled onions, and a secret sriracha mayo—a flavor explosion mirroring Dizzy's innovative bebop style. The "Billie Holiday Burger" was a melancholic masterpiece, a juicy patty cradled in a pretzel bun, draped with melty Swiss cheese and caramelized onions, a hint of sweetness amidst the savory, reflecting Billie's soulful voice.

The response was electric. Foodies with a penchant for the past flocked to "The Blues Burger Joint." The quirky menu items became conversation starters, and the playlists added a whole new dimension to the dining experience. People weren't just grabbing a burger; they were embarking on a musical journey with each bite.

Slowly but surely, the melody of Danny's business started to change. The once-hemorrhaging "Blues Burger Joint" was now a bustling hub, a testament to Danny's willingness to adopt Lean business practices. Danny "Fingers" Fontana had found a new rhythm, a delicious fusion of food, music, and the internet, proving that even in the twilight of his career, he could still create something beautiful, something that resonated with the audience.

TLDR: You can apply an antifragile mindset to business. The Lean Startup strategy is a good example of it.

Fail Your Way to Success

In this chapter, I've told stories about being fragile (Roderigo), being resilient (August), and being antifragile (Danny). Our control of others is limited (if not nonexistent), but we can control ourselves. We can only achieve GOAT World if all our minds are in peak performance.

HOW MUCH YOU LEARN

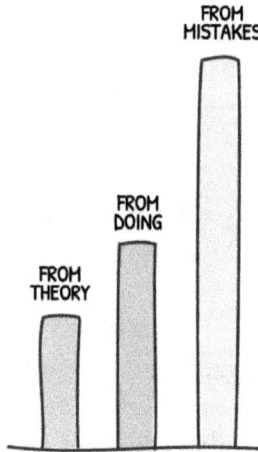

FROM
MISTAKES

FROM
DOING

FROM
THEORY

@JUNHANCHIN

Learning from mistakes is a common idea. We can choose to learn from mistakes, from experience, or from the lessons of others. We have to deal with failure and improvement almost daily. For example, your app constantly updates (sends bug fixes), whether you know it or not. The thesis of this chapter is that you can upgrade your mindset so that now even little errors help you thrive and grow.

Why It Would Work

- The body naturally overcompensates (via hormesis) to repair and strengthen itself.
- People can behave in ways that override their emotions.

What Will Happen

- People will grow because of "volatile" times, not despite them.
- Stronger people are more likely to explore ideas and the world.
- Everyone will be less hesitant to take calculated risks.
- An antifragile mindset will increase the likelihood of success in business endeavors.

Two Mysteries Solved

Rain lashed against the window, the rhythmic drumming a familiar lullaby to the old dog, Milo. Curled beside the fireplace, he watched the embers dance, their flickering glow painting memories on the backs of his eyelids. He remembered chasing butterflies as a pup, the exhilaration of the hunt, and the sweet scent of summer meadows clinging to his fur.

A twig snapped outside, pulling Milo from his reverie. Ears perked, he lifted his head, instantly recalling the countless times that sound meant a raccoon prowling for scraps. His body tensed, not in blind fear but in calculated caution. Years of experience had woven a tapestry of memories, each thread a past encounter, each knot a learned response.

He didn't need to see the raccoon to predict its next move. It would circle the house, drawn by the scent of dinner, then attempt an entry point—the back door, most likely. With a sigh, Milo thumped his tail against the floor, a preemptive warning.

His human, Sarah, stirred on the couch. "Something wrong, boy?" she mumbled, her voice thick with sleep.

Milo whined softly, his gaze fixed on the back door. Sarah followed his line of sight, understanding dawning in her eyes. She rose slowly, the familiar creak of the floorboards another thread in the vast tapestry of their shared memories.

Together, they moved as a unit, a silent symphony honed by experience. Sarah grabbed a flashlight, the beam a comforting presence in the dark. Milo crept towards the back door, using his knowledge of the house's layout to position himself for a strategic intercept.

The raccoon, as predicted, was there, its beady eyes reflecting the flashlight's beam. A growl rumbled from Milo's throat, a sound born not just of instinct but of the countless past confrontations that had taught him the language of dominance. The raccoon, recognizing the futility of its attempt, slunk away, melting back into the storm.

Milo relaxed, a satisfied rumble escaping his chest. He hadn't needed complex commands or spoken language. The dance between him and Sarah, the memories woven into their very being, had been enough. That quiet victory was a testament to countless shared experiences. There, in the powerful interplay of memory and prediction, flickered the essence of intelligence.

What Our Best Friends Can Teach of Intelligence

Milo's ability to react intelligently provides one of the most fundamental insights into intelligence. As we consider the growing impact of **artificial** intelligence on our everyday lives, we need to understand what makes something truly intelligent.

Current Machine Learning (ML) systems use the stimulus-response approach. They excel at rote tasks but cannot do high-level reasoning or anything that requires planning or novel problem-solving.

What is "real" intelligence? Is it simply a matter of complex behavior? Or is there something more to it? I believe the most convincing definition of intelligence was given by the co-creator of the Palm Pilot, Jeff Hawkins, who posits you need two things to be intelligent: memory and prediction.

Hawkins argues that the true definition of intelligence is not determined by how an organism acts. Instead, it's the ability to form memories of past experiences and use those memories to predict future outcomes.[4] This concept goes beyond just reacting to stimuli.

This reframing of intelligence has profound implications for our pursuit of machine learning and intelligence. Traditionally, ML has focused on mimicking complex human behaviors such as playing chess, translating languages, and recognizing objects. However, Hawkins' definition means we need to move beyond replicating actions and instead focus on building machines that can remember and predict. With this knowledge and understanding, we are much closer to building the next generation of artificial intelligence, which will allow us to create GOAT World.

For example, we could build tutors for everyone on the planet. We could build robotaxis that run 24/7 and can drive you anyplace, anytime. We could create an army of robot workers to build hospitals and robot doctors to fill them. We could build robots that clean the dishes, do the laundry, clean the house, and mow the lawn. The possibilities are nearly endless. But before we get too far ahead of ourselves, let me explain consciousness.

TLDR: Intelligence is not behavior; it's memory plus prediction.

Ben

The insistent trill of Ben's alarm ripped him from a dream of scaling a precariously balanced stack of breakfast buffets. Groaning, he fumbled for the offending device and silenced it.

Ben was a creature of habit. Shower, shave, and the same worn-in Oxford shirt. In the kitchen, the dance began—toast the bagel, a smear of plain cream cheese, then a dollop of ruby-red strawberry jelly. Next came the pantomime of whisking eggs, the sizzle as they met the hot oil. Coffee, dark and strong, brewed while he devoured his breakfast masterpiece.

Fueled by caffeine and carbs, Ben headed out the door. As he rounded a corner, a figure materialized from an alleyway, shrouded in a lab coat that seemed to defy the summer sun.

"Benjamin Davies?" the figure rasped, voice like sandpaper.

Ben stopped, surprised. "Uh, yeah, that's me," he replied cautiously.

The figure stepped closer, revealing a face dominated by outlandish goggles and a wild mane of white hair. "Splendid! A candidate for the Chronogastro Experiment!" the figure declared, brandishing a device that looked like a futuristic toaster crossed with a bicycle helmet.

Before Ben could react, the figure zapped him with a beam of light. A wave of nausea washed over him, then receded as abruptly as it came. Blinking, he stared at the scientist, who was now packing away his contraption.

"There," the scientist chirped, "memory of your breakfast successfully erased! Now, go forth and contribute to the advancement of scientific knowledge!"

Ben, utterly bewildered, mumbled a thanks and continued on his way.

Reaching his office, he was greeted by the usual morning banter. "Morning, Ben! Coffee?" Sarah, his co-worker, asked, holding up a steaming mug.

"Sure, thanks," Ben replied, accepting the mug. "Actually, I don't think I had breakfast this morning. Feeling a little rushed."

A chorus of surprised gasps filled the room. Ben froze— hadn't he just devoured his bagel masterpiece minutes ago? A strange sense of unreality washed over him. Had he dreamt the entire breakfast? Or was this some sort of elaborate prank?

It was a reminder, a quirky one to be sure, of the messy beauty of human experience. Memories, even the seemingly mundane ones like breakfast, were the building blocks of our day, our narrative.

Shrugging it off, Ben sipped his coffee, the bitterness strangely comforting.

TLDR: Our memories are a big part of our consciousness.

Consciousness Defined

A fundamental question has not yet been answered when trying to engineer machine intelligence: What is consciousness? We need to lock down the definition before we can progress because we need artificial intelligence to have some aspects of consciousness, but not necessarily all.

Hawkins proposed a definition that makes the most sense. Here's the gist:

There are four elements that combine to form consciousness: Self-model, memory, senses, and qualia.[5] A self-model is another way to describe self-awareness. It's basically an internal representation of yourself, your actions, and your place in the world. In a mental simulation, you are yet another object that can act and be acted upon.

Memory is the storage of input, i.e., people, places, things, experiences, symbols, etc.

Senses are the ability to perceive the world, whether through organs, cameras, microphones, or even even antennae. They are essential for navigating and interacting with your environment. Qualia is the subjective experience of things—the redness of a rose, the tang of a lime.

These factors easily apply to human consciousness. For example, when you go to sleep, you have almost no memory, sense, or self-awareness. Your qualia is limited to your dream world. We call this a state of unconsciousness. So, these elements accurately explain consciousness, but they also provide a perfect blueprint for creating synthetic consciousness.

Here's the beauty of this approach: We can focus on building these core functionalities without descending into the philosophical quagmire of consciousness. We can scale or throttle all the necessary aspects of consciousness until synthetic consciousness emerges in the state we've imagined. For example, our AI does not need a complete self-model or senses so it doesn't feel pain, but it can have enough to perform in a human-like fashion. In other words, we have an unproblematic formula for consciousness.

TLDR: We can build scaleable consciousness for our synthetic intelligence.

Architecting Synthetic Intelligence

Our fear of the dark has ancient roots. Imagine our primate ancestors roaming the savannahs and surviving the night's predators with their overpowering speed, strength, and fangs. What did we have to survive but each other and our intelligence?

The dark is a beast. It creeps, it crawls, it promises monsters. It's the unknown, vast and hungry. You hear rustles, creaks, and shadows dancing in the corners of your vision. Your mind, a fertile ground for fear, plants a garden of terrors.

Then, the click. A tiny burst of light, a defiant pinprick against the blackness. The flashlight beam is a sword, cutting through the darkness. The monsters retreat, revealed as mere shadows, illusions born of fear. The world, once a terrifying abyss, becomes a place to explore with vast new vistas to discover. The unknown is tamed.

Fast forward hundreds of thousands of years to today. Our civilization would be unimaginable without electricity: no lights, no refrigerators, no microwaves, no computers, no TVs, no phones—we'd give up almost everything we rely on every day!

It's a fundamental part of our lives now.

Similarly, SI is poised to become humanity's new electricity!

However, just as we prioritize safety for electricity, we must prioritize safety in developing something so history-changing as SI!

Ready for an Upgrade

The state of the art in current machine learning is Large Language Models (LLMs). The incredible usefulness of LLMs lies in their ability to process and generate massive amounts of text data, leading to a range of applications. Here are some examples:

- Revolutionizing Search Engines: LLMs can analyze vast amounts of text data, understand search queries with greater nuance, and surface more relevant and informative results. Search engines will be able to find the documents containing your keywords, synthesize the information, and provide human-like summaries.
- Enhanced Content Creation: LLMs can assist with content creation by generating any text from marketing copy and social media posts to poems and scripts. The results will be human-like.
- Personalized Learning: LLMs can personalize the learning experience by tailoring educational

materials to individual student needs and learning styles. For example, the online learning platform Khan Academy does exactly this with its Khanmigo system. LLMs can democratize this type of learning experience.

- Breaking Down Language Barriers: LLMs have the potential to revolutionize machine translation, enabling seamless communication across languages. Real-time translation tools will convert words and capture the nuances of meaning and cultural context.
- Code Generation: LLMs are being explored to generate code and translate natural language instructions into functional programming languages. This could significantly speed up the development process and democratize coding by making it more accessible to those without extensive programming experience.

At the same time, they have some major drawbacks. Here are some examples:

- Job displacement: This applies to machine learning in general. As technology becomes more sophisticated, it will make human labor expensive in comparison.
- "Black Box" Problem: It's hard to believe, but the inner workings of LLMs are cryptic and cannot be understood by humans. In my view, this is the biggest technical challenge that needs to be overcome.
- Hallucinations: Hallucinations refer to incorrect and nonsensical outputs that are irrelevant outputs to the input prompt. These outputs can appear grammatically correct and even plausible. For example, an LLM used to generate marketing copy might create content that is offensive or discriminatory.

- Lack of Planning and Certain Types of Reasoning: LLMs excel at processing and generating text, but they often lack the ability to understand the physical world or apply common-sense reasoning. This can lead to nonsensical or misleading outputs.[6]
- Bias and Discrimination: LLMs are trained on massive amounts of text data, which can reflect and amplify societal biases. This can lead to discriminatory outputs, for example, perpetuating stereotypes in generated content or producing biased search results.
- Misinformation and "Fake News": LLMs' ability to generate realistic-sounding text can be misused to create fake news articles or social media posts. The output's human-like quality can make it difficult to distinguish between genuine information and machine-generated content.

These are just a few examples of the potential and pitfalls of state-of-the-art machine learning. In my opinion, it is the most powerful technology invented by humankind. This means much thought, care, and humility must be used to advance and harness it.

Evelyn

Dr. Evelyn Walsh squinted at the swirling lines and nonsensical characters on her computer screen. She was trying to make sense of the hidden neurons from their latest machine learning-based diagnosis app. She'd poured years of research and a mountain of grant money into it. The promise: a medical diagnosis tool that could analyze patient data and identify diseases with unparalleled accuracy.

The reality? A frustrating black box. The app churned out results, some seemingly spot-on, others bafflingly wrong. But why? How? Peering into the inner workings of the so-called Artificial Neural Network (ANN) was like staring into a cosmic fog. The complex web of weighted connections and hidden layers offered no clear explanation for its decisions.

Evelyn wasn't naive. She knew ANNs were powerful tools capable of learning patterns invisible to the human eye. But this lack of transparency gnawed at her. It was like having a superpowered race car with a blind driver—it might get you somewhere fast but with no understanding of how. She was starting to realize the potential for disaster was too real.

Her frustration wasn't just academic. Imagine a doctor relying on an opaque system for a life-altering diagnosis. What if the ANN identified a rare disease in a patient, but the doctor couldn't verify the reasoning behind it? Trust, the cornerstone of the doctor-patient relationship, would crumble. More importantly, lives are at stake.

Evelyn wasn't ready to throw in the towel. Her new architecture would eventually not only make diagnoses but also explain their reasoning in a way humans could understand. She was excited to keep troubleshooting until the possibilities were real.

Upgrading to Synthetic Intelligence

The current technology in artificial intelligence is very good. In my experience, it can amplify productivity by many times. However, it has challenges, and we've already touched on them. I have condensed these into three problems, each of which I propose a solution to. Fundamentally, we must upgrade from artificial intelligence to synthetic intelligence (SI) because the current path is neither sustainable nor safe.

Challenge 1: Alignment

Due to the synthetic nature of this new form of intelligence, alignment with human values is not guaranteed. How can we ensure that synthetic intelligent agents' or systems' actions, goals, and values do not conflict with short or long-term human well-being? To illustrate the dangers, let me describe the famous Stamp Collector thought experiment. In this scenario, you instruct an AI capable of planning and executing your goal: collect as many stamps as possible. To achieve this goal, it kills all other stamp collectors and monopolizes all the stamps. It accomplished its goal but with horrifying consequences. We could always apply strict rules for every imaginable eventuality, but guardrails on artificial intelligence tend to be brittle because there are too many edge cases. Just look at the many ways people *can* and *do* jailbreak popular LLM-based systems. In this case, to trick the machine into explaining how to build a bomb, for example, you would feed it certain lines in order to "fool" it into giving you information for your malicious goals.

Solution 1: Foresight and Memory

The solution to the alignment problem is to give synthetic intelligence foresight (aka imagination). After all, humans have imaginations and have been socialized to use it to regulate our behaviors. So, first and foremost, synthetic intelligence must be able to answer the question: What are the consequences of this action? To do this, the system must have imagination (mental simulation).

I believe the future of synthetic intelligence isn't just about processing power and complex algorithms. It's about creating machines that can not only learn from data but also from our history, our mistakes, and our triumphs. It's about creating a future where AI isn't just a tool but a partner, one that shares our goals and understands the weight of its actions.

Challenge 2: Understandability and Explainability

For all their impressive feats, traditional machine learning (using artificial neural networks) operates as a black box. The systems churn out results with little transparency into the "how" behind their decisions. This lack of explainability is, in my opinion, the biggest challenge, especially in critical fields like medicine or defense. As in Evelyn's story, an accurate diagnosis is only so helpful if the system provides a rationale for that diagnosis.

Solution: Hierarchical Probabilities

We need to upgrade our architecture away from hidden layers to a probabilistic hierarchy, specifically, hierarchical probabilistic graph models (PGMs). Hierarchical PGMs break down components and assign probabilities to their relationships. This approach uses math similar to Google Page Rank.

For example, say you want to create synthetic intelligence to summarize books. We can use a hierarchy of books starting from the "building block" of words, which compose sentences, followed by paragraphs, chapters, and, finally, the book at the top of the hierarchy.

Hierarchy
of objects

book

chapters

paragraphs

sentences

words

Based on that hierarchy, I can create a more complex PGM that looks like this.

Probabilistic
relationships
of objects

book

chapters

paragraphs

sentences

words

Each level of the hierarchy becomes a node in the PGM. So, we'd have nodes for "book," "chapters," "paragraphs," and "words."

The connecting lines are called edges. They attach nodes and represent the probabilistic relationships between them.

For example, there would be an edge between "book" and "chapters," indicating the probability of a book containing chapters.

The hierarchical PGM is a powerful tool for understanding the statistical relationships between the elements. In fact, every natural system can be explained through a probabilistic hierarchy, which supports the idea that human intelligence uses a probabilistic approach. It has also been proven to work. Scientist Dileep George et al. have verified this idea by building AI with this concept.[7] So, if we use hierarchical PGMs to build synthetic intelligence, it will allow us to move beyond the hidden layers of ANNs and LLMs.

Challenge 3: Affordability

Currently, training an AI is like cramming for a test—you bombard it with every possible scenario. This is the status quo, and it uses the "stimulus-response" approach. It's thorough but expensive, requiring vast amounts of computing and electricity. For example, a state-of-the-art LLM can require anywhere between 150 to 285 kWh worth of electricity to train.[8] For comparison, a typical refrigerator uses between 0.3 to 0.8 kW, which is equivalent to anywhere between 500 and 900 refrigerators worth of electricity per hour.[9]

In my view, the current high cost of machine learning stifles creativity and healthy competition.

Solution: Rely on Mental Simulation

Yet again, the solution is imagination (mental simulation). Creating virtual worlds is a well-established and understood technology. By adding this key feature, synthetic intelligence doesn't need to be spoon-fed every answer, which can be resource-intensive. It can learn to generate its own solutions and explain its reasoning based on the simulated experiences.

This focus on simulation reduces the need for massive datasets and leads to more transparent and adaptable synthetic intelligence systems. In terms of cost, we can throttle or scale as needed. For example, we can tune any number of aspects in a simulation, such as world size, world resolution, max number of objects, object resolution, length size of simulation recording/persistence, max number of simulations to run, etc. Similarly, in the realm of automobile engineering, we use our understanding of the combustion engine to build go-karts or Formula One race cars, but now apply that same level of understanding to engineering intelligent machines!

Challenge	Description	Solution
Alignment	Ensuring AI goals align with human well-being	-Build SI with curiosity and a drive for truth-seeking -Provide SI with a diverse dataset encompassing human history (successes and failures)
Understandability and Explainability	Lack of transparency in AI decision-making due to hidden layers	Use hierarchical probabilistic graph models to break down problems and assign probabilities
Affordability	Expensive data requirements for traditional AI training	Include simulation (mental modeling) to explore possibilities and learn

In a GOAT World, human-aligned SI will be 100 percent understandable, explainable, and affordable to all.

To build even more safety, I propose a fourth ingredient: throttle capabilities. For example, we want to avoid building

Skynet. Why? Because giving total (or near-total) control of your nation's nuclear arsenal is an obviously unsafe design!

We have decades of engineering safety experience to inform this crucial issue. In my view, it should be top of mind as we develop and commit to SI.

This revolutionary technology holds the potential to unlock almost unimaginable possibilities, enabling us to tackle humanity's most difficult challenges with unprecedented precision and insight. By ensuring that SI systems are transparent and accessible, we can foster trust and collaboration, paving the way for innovations that could transform healthcare, education, our environment, and beyond. The future is bright with the promise of SI that works for everyone, everywhere.

SI as Electricity

We Fear the Dark

Our fear of the dark has ancient roots. Imagine our primate ancestors roaming the savannahs and surviving the night's predators with their overpowering speed, strength, and fangs. What did we have to survive but each other and our intelligence?

The dark is a beast. It creeps, it crawls, it promises monsters. It's the unknown, vast and hungry. You hear rustles, creaks, and shadows dancing in the corners of your vision. Your mind, a fertile ground for fear, plants a garden of terrors.

Then, the click. A tiny burst of light, a defiant pinprick against the blackness. The flashlight beam is a sword, cutting through the darkness. The monsters retreat, revealed as mere shadows, illusions born of fear. The world, once a terrifying abyss, becomes a place to explore with vast new vistas to discover. The unknown is tamed.

Fast forward hundreds of thousands of years to today.

Our civilization would be unimaginable without electricity: no lights, no refrigerators, no microwaves, no computers, no TVs, no phones... we'd give up almost everything we rely on every day!

It's a fundamental part of our lives now.

Similarly, SI is poised to become humanity's new electricity!

However, just as we prioritize safety for electricity, we must prioritize safety in developing something so history-changing as SI.

Even More Safety

To build even more safety, I propose a 4th ingredient: throttle capabilities. For example, we want to avoid building Skynet. Why? Because giving total (or near-total) control to your nation's nuclear arsenal is obviously an unsafe design.

We have decades of engineering safety experience to inform this crucial issue. In my view, it should be top of mind as we develop and commit to SI.

Electric Plug Safety as Inspiration

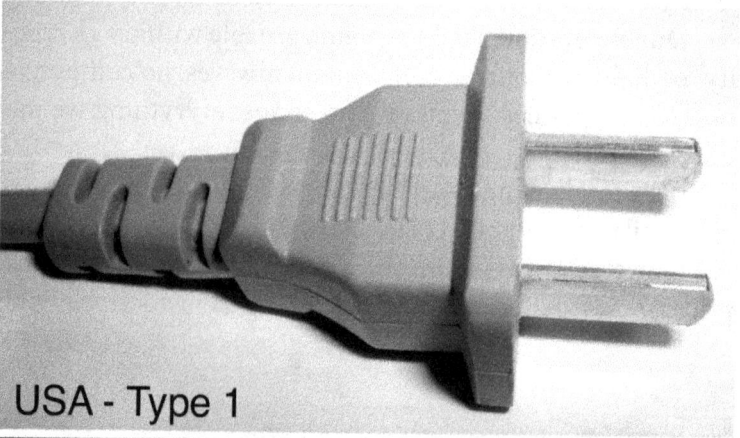

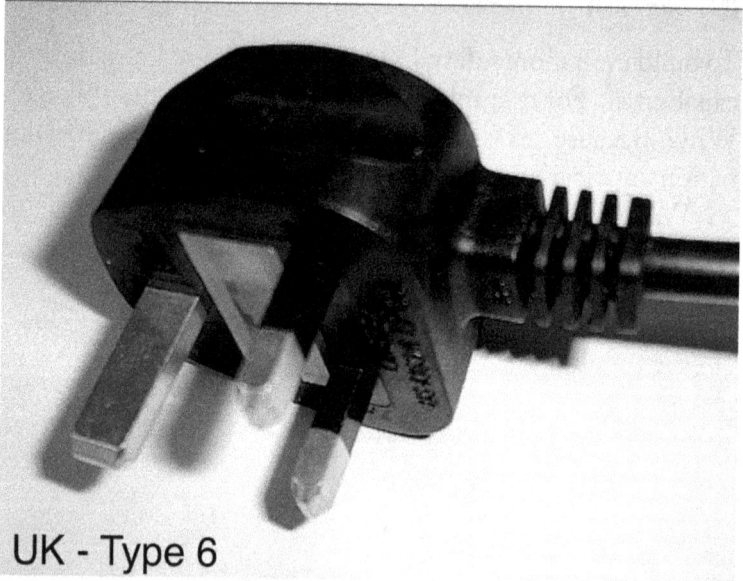

USA - Type 1

UK - Type 6

Source: https://travel.stackexchange.com/questions/4303/what-do-cuban-power-plugs-look-like

The United Kingdom has, arguably, designed the SAFEST electrical plug in the world. Why? Because they have more safety features built in to prevent accidental electrocution. How? First, if a child wants to poke an outlet, the outlets are blocked by a shutter which are closed by default and only opens when a plug is attached to the outlet. Second, the neutral and live leads of the plug have a plastic insulation over half of them, so you cannot put your fingers on a live wire while it is plugged in. Lastly, each plug has a built-in fuse, which usually means each individual appliance has a dedicated fuse for it. Individual fuses per appliance are better than circuit-breakers that generally only protect rooms, which is good, but not as capable as per-device protection against overloads or short circuits.

TLDR: Throttle SI capabilities for extra safety.

Why It Would Work

- Every natural system can be described as a probabilistic hierarchy.
- Dileep George et al. have already built and productized AI systems using this approach.
- Malice and ill will are not necessarily part of intelligence.

What Will Happen

- We will create human-aligned AI that is 100 percent understandable, explainable, and affordable to all.
- Unlock almost unimaginable possibilities for solving humanity's most complex challenges.

Implications

isha tapped her finger impatiently on the worn desk, the dusty textbook offering little to ignite her curiosity. The classroom hummed with a monotonous drone as the teacher recited facts in a monotone. Aisha yearned for deeper understanding, for connections that resonated beyond rote memorization.

Then, whispers emerged about Project Euclid, an SI program designed to revolutionize education. When Aisha received her Luminaid—a sleek device that projected directly into her visual cortex—skepticism lingered. Yet, as Euclid began its lessons, the classroom walls dissolved.

Euclid wasn't a mere facts dispenser; it was a living library with infinite patience. It analyzed Aisha's learning patterns, crafting immersive simulations that transported her to ancient civilizations. SI simulations of historical figures engaged her in lively debates, while personalized learning modules filled knowledge gaps identified by Euclid's vast intelligence.

Aisha flourished. History became a vibrant tapestry woven with the threads of human experience. Euclid helped her unearth hidden connections, predict potential outcomes of events, and even compose an award-winning historical fiction piece with an uncanny level of historical accuracy. Years later, Aisha stood before a captivated audience, not as a product of rote learning but as a testament to the power of SI-empowered education. "Project Euclid," she proclaimed, "ushered in an era where the collective wisdom of humanity became a tool to unlock the potential within every mind."

TLDR: Synthetic intelligence that is affordable to all means personal tutors for every person on the planet

Elias

Elias entered the world an anomaly, a testament to the unexpected turns nature could take. Born with a rare genetic glitch, he lacked the very limbs that defined the human experience – no arms, no legs, just a torso and a head. Yet, within that seemingly limited frame, a spark of consciousness flickered, a testament to the boundless potential of the human mind.

His early years were a blur of assistance and adaptation. Medical technology, propelled by the relentless hum of synthetic intelligence, offered a glimmer of hope. 3D printing, a technology once relegated to crafting prototypes, had taken a revolutionary leap forward, allowing for the creation of organic tissues. For Elias, this meant the possibility of limbs, not robotic extensions, but living, breathing parts seamlessly integrated with his own body.

His journey, however, wasn't a fairytale. There were setbacks and moments of frustration, where the limitations of the nascent technology gnawed at his spirit. Each failed attempt, each rejection by his body, pushed the boundaries of science, forcing the SI algorithms to refine and the bioprinting techniques to adapt. Slowly, painstakingly, his body began to accept the printed limbs, integrating them into his being.

He ran marathons, went on long walks with his children, danced with his wife, and climbed mountains. He yearned to feel the sun on his skin and the wind in his hair, experiences forever denied to him by his unique biology. The richness of the mind, the boundless potential of human connection.

TLDR: We can harness synthetic intelligence to solve humanity's difficult challenges, including all forms of medical maladies.

Robolabor

The whirring symphony of the automated assembly line was a far cry from the clanging, back-breaking, grimy factories of yesteryear. Here, in the gleaming heart of the MegaTech facility, robots with clockwork precision assembled next-generation gadgets at blinding speed. It was a future straight out of science fiction, and the benefits were undeniable.

Elsewhere, robots took over all three D's (Dirty, Dangerous, and Drugery work). Many essential jobs fell under these. The rise of synthetic intelligence fundamentally reshaped this landscape. Grueling labor in mines, toxic waste processing, and mind-numbing assembly line tasks were the unfortunate realities for a large swathe of the human workforce but were now taken over by robots.

The new workforce tirelessly churned out identical products on assembly lines, freeing humans from the monotony of repetitive tasks. This shift wasn't just about safety and efficiency; it was about unlocking human potential. By taking over the less-than-desirable jobs, robots allowed us to pursue our interests, ushering in an era where creativity, problem-solving, and innovation took center stage.

Also, people were now free to spend their time with loved ones, travel, learn new skills, and pursue creative endeavors like sculpting or dancing.

TLDR: Harnessing synthetic intelligence would allow near-limitless labor, free up time, and create incredible material wealth.

Would Robots Be Slaves?

This is an important and valid question, especially since consciousness and intelligence are now understood well enough to build SI assistants as capable as human beings.

Would it be ethical to treat and use them like they were inanimate objects if they were intelligent?

I think the best way to think about and answer this ethical question is an analogy. In the popular anime *Cells at Work*, the human body is a city and the various cells are anthropomorphized as characters. For example, red blood cells are depicted as people wearing red hats and red overalls. Each episode is about how the different characters respond to emergencies in the town (human body)—various ailments like food poisoning or the common cold. The show drives the point that our bodies rely on countless uncomplaining cells to function. We have no ethical grievances with their fates because they are not conscious. The thought never even crosses our minds.

Similarly, could SI become a seamless extension of humanity, serving without sentience, emotion, or suffering?

Yes. The ethics of owning robots and having them do our bidding are analogous to the cells in our bodies. We will build SI so we determine their capabilities and limitations. They need not have self-awareness—there is no reason they have to, according to our scaleable model of consciousness. They would not experience pain or any form of suffering, real or imagined.

So, just as our bodies rely on and thrive on a diverse range of biological automata, we can now propel humanity to even greater heights with SI automata!

Preparing for the Journey

If we upgrade current Machine Learning to my proposed architecture for Synthetic Intelligence, we will have a clear path to eliminate poverty, hunger, disease, war, and nearly all human ailments.

We can engineer supercells without the baggage of malice, pain, or suffering. This can happen if we create SI that is human-aligned, completely explainable and understandable, and affordable to all.

PART 2

Playing Our Cards Right

*You can get through it **if** you **believe** you can get through it.*
The mind is a strong muscle.
—Ms. Pat

See reality. Bend reality.
—Garry Tan

"Where are you going, fool? The only green you'll find is envy!" the other goats taunted.

Joaquin ignored them, his resolve hardening with each step. Finally, he reached the wooden bridge, a rickety contraption swaying over a dizzying chasm. Fear clawed at him. He'd never been so high, and the bridge seemed ready to crumble at the slightest touch. Yet, the memory of the emerald dream spurred him on.

Slowly, Joaquin inched across the bridge. Every creak sent shivers down his spine. He closed his eyes, picturing the green valley, the taste of sweet grass. Just as doubt threatened to overwhelm him, he felt...

Preamble

Yusuf swiveled in his chair, the fluorescent lights of the conference room glinting off his bald head. A gaggle of young developers, their faces flushed with the fervor of youth, presented their latest project: a next-generation social media platform guaranteed to revolutionize user engagement. Their voices echoed with a familiar refrain, "Open-source it all! Let the collective mind of the Internet build the future of connection!"

Yusuf, the company's CEO and a veteran of the tech wars, couldn't help but admire their unbridled enthusiasm. Open-source software had become the tech world's golden goose—a symbol of radical collaboration and accelerated innovation. However, open-sourcing everything wasn't a magic spell that worked for every project.

"Hold on a beat, team," Yusuf interjected, his voice calm but firm. "Open-source is a beautiful thing, but let's not get carried away. This platform has the potential to be disruptive, and let's be honest, some of those algorithms are our secret sauce." He explained the delicate dance they needed to perform. Open-sourcing core functionalities could ignite a wave of creative contributions, but exposing their proprietary algorithms could leave them defenseless against copycats.

A thoughtful hush fell over the room. Yusuf wasn't advocating for a cloistered approach. He envisioned a hybrid model—a meticulously curated open-source ecosystem where developers could contribute to specific features without jeopardizing their competitive edge. It wasn't the naive "build it and they will come" mindset. It was a more nuanced strategy that embraced collaboration while safeguarding their intellectual property.

Open-source software was a powerful tool, but like any tool, it needed to be wielded with strategic foresight and a keen understanding of its limitations. In the ever-shifting tech landscape, sometimes the most groundbreaking ideas emerge from striking the right balance between collaboration and calculated secrecy.

TLDR: Open-sourcing all software code would be too harmful. State secrets and privacy algorithms, for example, are protected for good reason.

Liam and Nadia

As the snow fell, Nadia gazed through the window, lost in thought. Liam, her partner of seven years, sat across from her, wondering what she was thinking about. They'd been discussing their relationship, a conversation that had been circling for months. Liam, ever the explorer, had recently brought up ethical non-monogamy, a concept that left Nadia feeling adrift.

"Is this the future?" she choked out, the words catching in her throat. Images of sitcom portrayals and scandalous headlines filled her mind. "Are we supposed to be…evolved because we're open to this?"

Liam shook his head, his touch gentle on her hand. "No, love. It's not a competition. ENM isn't some badge of honor. It's just…different."

Nadia scoffed. "Different how? Different from the love we've built together?"

Liam sighed. "It doesn't have to be a dismantling of what we have. It could be an expansion. We could still have our commitment and intimacy, but maybe we could explore connections outside our relationship, too."

Nadia thought back to an article she'd read, a woman who'd practiced ENM for years. The author stressed it wasn't ideal for everyone. "But what if it's not for us? What if it breaks everything?"

Liam squeezed her hand. "Then we stop. There's no shame in that. There's no 'better' kind of love, Nadia. We just need to figure out what feels right for us."

Silence settled between them, heavy with uncertainty. Maybe there was no ideal. Maybe with eight billion different people, thinking there was only one way they'd be happy in a relationship seemed far-fetched. Maybe, just maybe, the answer wasn't some pre-defined model but a path they had to forge together, hand in hand, navigating the storm one careful step at a time.

TLDR: Ethical non-monogamy (ENM) is not the ideal relationship style for everybody. It is just another choice for informed, consenting adults.

Is This the Future?

In "Setting the Pieces," I defined intelligence, consciousness, and what it means to upgrade to an antifragile mindset. Last, I described a way to make SI that is human-aligned, explainable, and affordable to all.

We covered a lot. But even with the pieces in place, we still have to play our cards right. The relentless march of technology presents us with staggering possibilities and nightmare scenarios. While it can transform lives for the better, it can also leave people in our communities behind. For some, the damage is temporary; for others, it is permanent and devastating. Not everyone has the resources to weather the storm. Can you imagine yourself in their situation?

Furthermore, developed countries face unique problems, such as declining birth rates and rising divorce rates.

Developing countries can "leap ahead" by adopting mostly mature and proven tech from the developed world. For example, the cost of essential resources like housing and farming equipment can create a barrier to entry for many.

The challenges are big, so we need novel, bold solutions. We need to implement open-source models, the freedom dividend, and ethical non-monogamy (ENM).

Here, I present plans to help bridge us to The Endgame. However, these actions must be taken first before we reach GOAT World.

Open Source Ecology

Marcin squinted at the endless rows of wheat, his calloused hand tracing a hesitant line down a stalk. The city life, once a vibrant dream, now felt like a faded photograph compared to the earthy canvas stretching before him. He was a farmer now, a decision fueled by a yearning for simpler things, not a fat bank account.

His pride and joy, a rusty but rumbling tractor named Bertha, chugged along the furrows, leaving behind a trail of freshly turned soil. The joy of seeing life sprout where there was only dust was a balm to his soul. Until, with a sputter and a cough, Bertha lurched to a stop. Panic clawed at Marcin's throat. He had barely scraped together enough to buy the darn thing, let alone repairs.

Days turned into weeks as Marcin nursed Bertha back to health, every penny he'd saved going towards the mechanic. He worked tirelessly by hand, his back aching, sweat stinging his eyes, but the thought of his wife, Elara, and their two young children with empty plates spurred him on.

Just as hope flickered back, a sickening crunch shattered the morning quiet. Bertha, spewing smoke, refused to budge. Despair threatened to engulf Marcin. He stared at the endless fields, the dream turning into a nightmare. How would he feed his family? How could he explain this to Elara, her eyes already etched with worry?

That evening, Elara placed a steaming bowl of stew in front of him. Her smile, though strained, held a strength that mirrored the wheat swaying in the breeze. "We'll figure it out," she said, her voice firm.

TLDR: The status quo is planned obsolescence. Not everyone can afford the newest, best, or even unexpected repairs.

Democratizing Resources: Open Source for Food and Shelter

For the developing world, the cost of essential resources like farming equipment and housing materials creates a barrier to self-sufficiency for many.

What if we could implement the open-source models used in software for hardware? Imagine a world where the blueprints for a circuit board and the intricate plans for a 3D printer weren't so unaffordable to so many. Just like with software, the design schematics and manufacturing instructions would be freely available. Anyone with a passion and a soldering iron could contribute, modify, and improve upon existing designs. Open-source models offer a novel solution.

Enter the Open Source Ecology (OSE) project, which attempts to harness the power of the open-source approach by making the plans for our society freely available and accessible. They call it the Global Village Construction set.

It includes plans for tractors, backhoes, 3D printers, and more. By sharing designs and blueprints freely, individuals and communities can manufacture their own tools and shelters at a significantly lower cost.[10]

Could open-sourcing hardware work? Let's step back to see the most famous example of open-source success.

Linux

The entire Internet infrastructure is run mostly by the open-source operating system (OS) Linux. Its significance is undeniable. How did we get here, and could it work for hardware?

Linux wasn't an overnight success story. It is a project with roots that burrow back to the 1980s. Back then, Richard Stallman, a visionary hacker, embarked on a project he called GNU (which stands for GNU's Not Unix). His audacious goal? To create a free and open-source operating system, a rebellion against the proprietary giants like Unix that dominated at the time. The GNU Project became popular and spawned essential tools and utilities, the building blocks of a revolutionary OS. But there was a missing piece, the heart of the operating system—the kernel.

Fast forward to 1991, and enter Linus Torvalds, a Finnish student who was young, brash, and confident in his skills. He wasn't consumed by building the next big thing, though; he just wanted a free Unix-like kernel for his own machine. What he created, however, resonated with a global audience. The magic of Linux lies in its open-source nature. Unlike its closed-sourced counterparts, anyone could tinker, modify, and distribute the kernel freely since the source was in the public domain. This unleashed a global army of developers.

Each contributor brought a unique perspective, and Linux evolved into a powerful, versatile OS.

Today, Linux dominates the server landscape, the invisible engine powering everything from routers to supercomputers. It even lurks beneath the hood of Android smartphones, a testament to its adaptability.

Why Open Source Ecology?

What's so special about open-source methods? First, they democratize innovation. Resource-constrained inventors, who have little or no resource and development budgets, can tap into a global knowledge base and collaborate on projects that might have otherwise remained mere pipe dreams.

Second, it fosters rapid iteration. Unlike the slow, siloed processes of traditional hardware development, OSE allows for swift improvements and bug fixes as a **distributed community** puts the design through its paces. Think of it as a constant beta test fueled by the collective ingenuity of the maker movement.

Given the above, OSE is brimming with potential. Imagine a future where the schematics for complex robots or the blueprints for next-generation solar panels are freely available, empowering a global network of tinkerers and problem-solvers. With that, the future promises abundance for all, one open-source project at a time.

Why It Would Work

- Open-source software already runs our infrastructure.
- More eyes means more opportunities to find bugs.
- The nature of OSE allows for rapid improvement.

- Availability in the public domain creates the potential to modify for specific use.

What Will Happen

- People will no longer have to worry about planned obsolescence.
- Freely available plans would allow developing nations to have the best technology.
- OSE would allow foundational technologies to be improved.

The Freedom Dividend

The tide of technological progress has always had a way of washing away the familiar. From the clatter of horseshoes replaced by the engine noise of automobiles to the rhythmic clack of typewriters silenced by the hum of computers, it seems to never end. Today, on the greasy floor of his auto repair shop, Edward grapples with the next wave—the rise of electric cars and the ominous whisper of robots capable of replacing even skilled mechanics.

A pang of unease settles in his gut as he examines a sleek electric car hoisted on the hydraulic lift. The diagnostic tools in his hand, once comforting extensions of his expertise, feel strangely cold. "Electric this, autonomous that," he mutters, wiping a stray bit of grease from his forehead. The future, once a distant horizon, seems to be barreling down on him like a runaway truck.

Across the garage, his son Ethan, a whirlwind of youthful enthusiasm, disassembles an old drone with the practiced ease of a seasoned explorer. He glances up, catching his eye, a mischievous glint in his gaze. "Speaking of robots, Dad, did you see that article about the self-repairing bots they're testing?" he asks.

TLDR: Technological changes seem to come quickly. Young people are more likely to pick up and adopt them.

Dizzying Pace

The pace of technological change can feel dizzying. Like a toddler discovering a room full of toys, we keep stumbling upon new gadgets and ideas at an ever-increasing rate. This rapid shift can be overwhelming, but it also opens up amazing possibilities. For instance, think about the difference between a clunky rotary phone and the smartphone in your pocket, a constant portal to information and connection. Technology can help us reach new heights or nightmare scenarios.

The key lies in approaching technology with idealism and pragmatism. We should celebrate the incredible progress that has improved our lives in countless ways. At the same time, we must acknowledge the potential downsides and work towards developing safeguards and frameworks to prevent, avoid, or mitigate them.

The Smiths

The delivery app glowed accusingly on the Smiths' kitchen counter. Takeout Tuesdays were a tradition, a refuge from the relentless pressure cooker of life. But tonight, the usual banter between Sandra and Michael was muted. Sandra, a freelance web developer, had just finished a particularly dry spell. Michael, a mechanic whose skills were increasingly challenged by electric vehicles, stared out the window, his brow furrowed. The specter of financial insecurity hung heavy in the air.

"Imagine," Sandra began, her voice barely a whisper, "a world where a quiet month wouldn't mean scrambling for bills."

Michael turned, a flicker of hope battling the cynicism that had become a familiar companion.

"A safety net," Sandra continued, the words carrying a newfound weight. "A chance to breathe, to explore new areas, maybe even take that pottery class you've always mentioned."

Michael, a man whose hands had always found solace in the tangible, harbored a secret desire—shaping clay into something beautiful.

The freedom dividend wasn't a novel concept. Wouldn't it stifle innovation? Wouldn't people become complacent? But as Sandra dug deeper, a new perspective emerged. What if the dividend wasn't a hammock but a launching pad? "I could start that pastry business I've always wanted," she thought.

The fear of losing their jobs wouldn't disappear, but the terror of freefall might. So, the takeout debate remained undecided, but a different kind of menu had opened—a menu of possibilities.

TLDR: Technological changes are coming fast and hard. The freedom dividend can be used to prevent permanent damage. It depends on the person.

The Freedom Dividend: Net, Fertilizer, and Soil

What is the Freedom Dividend? It was 2020 US presidential candidate Andrew Yang's signature proposal during his campaign. It is a universal payment of $1,000 per month to all American adults as a solution to the inevitable consequences of dizzying technological improvements leaving people behind.[11]

The five most common jobs in the United States are in administrative and clerical work, retail or sales, food service and prep, transportation, and manufacturing. They account for about half of all jobs in America.[12]

Percentage of jobs replaced by
automation/robots

If you believe robots and AI will become good enough to replace human labor, if you believe that technology will develop faster than people can go back to school or retrain, and if you believe not everyone has the money or time to do that, then the freedom dividend would be a safety net. Let me explain.

Automation and robot labor are coming online and will undoubtedly create staggering wealth. It can also leave many in our communities behind and render their skill sets useless. This creates a crucial need for a safety net—a system like The Freedom Dividend that ensures hard times don't cripple you.

The Freedom Dividend is like fertilizer and soil. Why? By ensuring that all citizens have their basic needs met with a guaranteed payment, regardless of employment status, the freedom dividend can prevent permanent damage from unexpected emergencies, hard times, and constant economic stress. It empowers individuals to pursue education, retrain for new jobs, or even start their own businesses. This allows and encourages innovation and entrepreneurship even in the face of technological disruption.

TLDR: Not everyone has the same amount of resources. The Freedom Dividend would give a helping hand, prevent hardship from the uncontrollable, and empower people to pursue entrepreneurial endeavors.

Criticisms of the Freedom Dividend

The first criticism of the Freedom Dividend is that, because you're giving people money, it will raise food prices, rent, and property values. The counterargument is that all you have to do is look at the computers from the 1980s versus your iPhone from right now. At first, computers cost millions of dollars and took up an entire room, whereas now you have computers that you put in your pocket.

The point is that technology is massively deflationary. Whatever inflation you get from helping people pay for their medicine, rent, child care, etc., is massively cancelled by the fact that robots will be unlimited labor.

The second criticism is that giving people $1,000 will be a disincentive for them to work. Well, people want to work. If the robots take the jobs, what choice do they have?

The other criticism is that we can't afford to pay people in an emergency. My argument is that we had a pandemic as an emergency, and we gave people money. Of course we can afford it.

I want to be clear: this is just a stopgap. It is not permanent! The permanent solution is to marry emotional and material currency. See End Game for a more in-depth explanation.

Why It Would Work

- People are struggling, and they want a solution.
- Not everybody has their basic needs taken care of.
- Not everybody is healthy enough to make a lot of money.
- The country is awash with money.[13]
- We have already provided safety nets, so this move is not unprecedented.

What Will Happen

- We will prevent permanent damage to our communities.
- People will be free to start businesses.
- It will remove stress from everyone.

Ethical Non-Monogamy

*L*ove is *Blind* is a popular dating show on Netflix. Singles in sleek, soundproof pods pour their hearts out, forging connections based solely on their conversation. Here's the catch: it was all or nothing. You get one "yes" to find you one true love.

Felicity, a woman who thrived on lists and spreadsheets, felt the absurdity of it all gnaw at her. Tears welled up in her eyes as Henry's voice, smooth and captivating, echoed through the pod speakers. "Did you already say yes to him?" The question hung heavy, a tangible weight in the air-conditioned silence.

She'd fallen for two men. Will, with his infectious laugh and encyclopedic knowledge of 90s trivia, had sparked a comfortable warmth. Then came Henry, a whirlwind of philosophical musings and travel dreams, painting vivid pictures of adventures yet to be had. Both connections felt real, a kaleidoscope of emotions that defied the show's rigid binary.

A choked sob escaped her lips. "Yeah," she croaked into the microphone, hating the vulnerability raw in her voice. This wasn't part of the plan. The experiment, designed to bypass the superficial, had thrown her into the emotional deep end. Here she was, a woman who thrived on control, grappling with the messy, unpredictable nature of love—a multifaceted gem, not a neatly categorized box.

A tense silence followed. Then, the familiar lilt of Henry's voice, heavy with disappointment. "Okay," he said, fighting from choking. "Congrats, you two."

The weight of the decision pressed down on her. Guilt coiled in her stomach. She longed to explain, to somehow navigate the uncharted territory of double connections. But the rules were clear. This was a one-shot gamble, a leap of faith into the unknown.

Henry's voice filled the pod again, laced with a hint of desperation. "If I went first, would you have said yes to me?"

Felicity threw herself back onto the pod chair, burying her face in her hands. Tears streamed down her cheeks, hot and silent. She couldn't answer. The question exposed the very heart of the problem—the experiment's rigid structure clashed with the messy reality of human connection.

TLDR: Humans are capable of loving more than one person at a time.

At the Heart of the Problem (Pun Intended)

Most likely, the cause of population collapse in developed countries is that women today must choose between building a career now or raising a family.[14] They are put in this predicament because of biological realities, societal expectations, and economic forces.[15] In my view, each plays a role, and different countries have varying degrees of each. Let's review all three.

While advancements in assisted reproduction technology offer some flexibility, they can't fully erase the biological reality: a woman's fertility rate begins a gradual decline in her late twenties and then takes a sharper dip after thirty-five. By her mid-forties, a woman's chances of natural conception become very low.

So, for women, the "prime" years for establishing themselves professionally, acquiring skills and experience, and climbing the career ladder coincide with the peak window for fertility.

Pregnancy and childbirth are time-consuming and resource-intensive enough, even more so if we want to raise happy, healthy, and well-adjusted humans.

Also, depending on a country's societal mores and norms for gender roles, women are expected to take the primary role in the household. Specifically, who should do the cooking, cleaning, household chores, and child-rearing?

Finally, economic realities often stack the deck against mothers. These realities—high cost of living, stagnant wages, and a lack of affordable childcare options—make raising children a financial strain.[16] This situation is well known and cannot be fixed quickly.

All the above forces create a predicament for women: whether to spend time and energy building a career or raising a family. Men do not have to face such a decision.

The solution to this big challenge involves two parts: upgrading how we think about romantic love and upgrading our socioeconomic system. I will describe the first part in this section and the second half in the next section.

TLDR: The likely root cause of population collapse is that women are put in a predicament to choose between career and family.

The Most Challenging Things Can Be the Most Rewarding

We understand that having high difficulty is just one way to provide an intense feeling of accomplishment through preparing strategies, overcoming obstacles, and discovering new things.
—Hitedataka Miyezaki, FromSoftware

In a typical video game, there are three difficulty levels: easy, medium, and hard. In a Souls game (series of games made by FromSoftware), there's only one difficulty: F*** you.

Why? Here are a couple of reasons.

This singular level of challenge is not merely a gimmick. It is a deliberate design choice that yields profound rewards. The arduous tasks, the seemingly insurmountable obstacles, force players to adapt, to learn from their mistakes, and to develop a deep understanding of the game's mechanics. The satisfaction that comes from overcoming such challenges is unparalleled. It is a triumph of skill, perseverance, and a touch of luck.

By focusing on a single difficulty level, game designers are freed from the constraints of balancing multiple modes. Now, they can devote their energies to crafting intricate enemies, stunning environments, and unique weapons. The result is a more immersive and rewarding experience for those who are willing to embrace the challenge.

However, it is important to acknowledge that this extreme level of difficulty is not for everyone. The Souls games appeal to a specific audience. For others, the relentless punishment can be frustrating and discouraging. It is a double-edged sword, offering immense satisfaction to some while alienating others.

What Is Ethical Non-Monogamy?

ENM, which encompasses open relationships, is a relationship structure where partners agree to have romantic or intimate relationships with people outside of the primary couple. However, unlike cheating, ENM is based on **open communication, consent,** and **clear boundaries.**

I want to be clear: adopting an ENM style of relationships is optional. Also, in my experience, the biggest factors in a successful relationship are communication, empathy, attraction, thoughtfulness, and patience. In my view, upgrading our mindsets and communication skills and emphasizing their importance is the most important factor for successful romantic relationships. ENM is the best example of this.

Imagine the level of communication it takes with multiple romantic partners. Can it be done? Yes. People have done it for years.[17]

While ENM might seem like an outlier, it is just another type of relationship, albeit more effortful. Let's look at the inherent challenges and benefits.

Challenges

Vulnerability. This is the core of genuine, deep connections. When you leave yourself open to being said "no" to, reprimanded, scolded, made fun of, or even humiliated, you risk so much. Why? Because now your ego and self-worth can be attacked. However, is there any other way to realize your most personal desires with those you love? Also, partners build incredible trust and deep understanding by working through the "hard conversations" together.

Jealousy. ENM requires a high degree of emotional maturity and self-awareness. This is because partners must confront and address jealousy. Jealousy is a signal of two things: insecurity and unfulfilled needs. Partners can only begin to resolve this by being open and honest about jealousy when inevitably arises.

Social acceptance. To say that ENM is a fringe relationship style would not be an exaggeration.[18] ENM still faces societal stigma, which can create strain on couples and their support networks. Navigating this stigma requires additional emotional resilience.

Benefits

ENM has the potential to enhance the quality of your connections. Here are a few reasons why.

Enhanced communication and conflict resolution. Having to resolve jealousy forces partners to become good at communication and conflict resolution. These skills can be used to strengthen your other relationships.

More time and resources. Contrary to popular belief, ENM can create more breathing room, not less. Why? Because now you don't have to be *everything* for *everyone.* In other words, parenting, caretaking, and even finances are shared across more loving humans. After an initial increase in upfront investment in time and resources, rather than competing for those resources, partners can become co-creators of stability and shared abundance.

Stronger support network. ENM can also unlock a treasure chest of support. Imagine a constellation of connections, each offering a unique source of friendship, guidance, and emotional sustenance.

Greater sexual and emotional needs fulfilled. Finally, let's not forget the potential for a richer tapestry of experiences. Imagine the possibility of exploring diverse desires and finding intimacy in ways that a single partner might not be able to fully satisfy. This exploration need not diminish the primary relationship; instead, it can lead to a more well-rounded and fulfilling emotional life.

The Bottom Line: ENM is not a magic bullet. The success of these partnerships hinges on emotional maturity, a commitment to growth, and the ability to navigate societal stigma. It's not for everyone.

Lastly, whether ENM becomes mainstream remains to be seen. History, however, points to yes.

We've Seen This Movie Before

The concept of normalcy is fascinatingly fluid. Behaviors once deemed deviant and relegated to the fringes of society have become commonplace as the world embraces the range of human experience. The following table shows once-deviant behavior as part of our cultural norms.

Let's briefly recap once-taboo cultural phenomena, revisiting activities that were once met with raised eyebrows but now wouldn't cause anyone to bat an eye.

Body Art: From the rebellious sailors sporting intricate tattoos to the self-expression of dyed hair, body modifications were once seen as a mark of deviance. Today, tattoos are a mainstream art form, adorning bodies of all ages and professions, a testament to our evolving definition of beauty.

Love Without Borders: Interracial relationships, once illegal in some places and frowned upon in many others, have become a beautiful reflection of our globalized world. Love stories defy borders, celebrating the richness that comes from embracing diversity.

The Power of Pants: Imagine a world where women couldn't wear pants! Shocking as it may seem, trousers were once deemed "masculine" attire. Thankfully, practicality and a shift in societal norms paved the way for pants to become a staple in any woman's wardrobe.

The Devil's Music: Rock and roll, with its rebellious spirit and loud guitars, sent shockwaves through the 1950s. Now, it's a genre celebrated for its energy and innovation, a reminder that sometimes, the most disruptive forces can become the most beloved.

The Joy of Movement: From the swirling waltzes of the past to the pulsating beats of today's clubs, dancing has faced its fair share of criticism. Yet, the primal urge to move our bodies transcends cultural boundaries, reminding us of the universal language of joy and expression.

A Toast (in Moderation): Today, responsible drinking is a part of many cultures, a reminder that even "deviant" behaviors can be enjoyed in moderation. Also, remember that our country had a dramatic and tumultuous time during The Prohibition Era.

The Green Debate: Marijuana, demonized for decades, is now finding acceptance for both medical and recreational uses. This shift reflects a growing openness to explore alternative treatments and redefine our relationship with psychoactive substances.

Behavior	Current Status	Time Period Considered Deviant
Women Wearing Pants	Common and fashionable clothing choice for women	19th Century (seen as improper attire for women)
Rock and Roll	Mainstream genre of music	1950s (seen as rebellious and potentially corrupting)
Dancing	Popular social activity and form of artistic expression	Varied throughout history (sometimes banned due to religious beliefs)
Alcohol Use	Legal and socially accepted for adults in moderation (can still be problematic)	Varied throughout history (religious restrictions, temperance movements)
Tattoos	Widely accepted form of body art	18th-19th Centuries
Homosexuality	Legal and increasingly accepted in many parts of the world	Throughout history, criminalized in many places
Interracial Relationships	Legal and increasingly accepted in many parts of the world	18th-20th Century (illegal or socially unacceptable in many places)
Marijuana Use (Medical & Recreational)	Legal for medical and/or recreational use in a growing number of countries (still illegal in many others)	20th-21st Century (criminalized in many places)
ENM	More openly discussed and practiced, though not universally accepted	Varies by culture (often seen as immoral or sinful)

These are just a few examples of how societal norms have shifted to embrace once-deviant behaviors. We've seen this pattern before. It will likely be accepted like so many of our once-taboo cultural mores and norms.

Can You Raise Happy, Healthy Children in an ENM Environment?

The honest answer: it remains to be seen.

Specifically, we don't yet have long-term, large-scale studies on children raised in ENM families the way we do non-traditional families like interracial or same-sex households (which were once considered deviant by popular culture). However, there are three things we know are true.

First, we know children need safety and stability. That means reliable routines, emotionally available caregivers, and environments where they don't have to guess whether they're secure, loved, or supported. Stability isn't necessarily about traditionalism; it's about **predictability**, **presence**, and **care**.

Second, Popular culture still considers ENM deviant. That stigma doesn't just affect adults; it creates a social environment where children may face confusion, shame, or exclusion, not because of harm within their family, but because of the bias outside of it.

Lastly, what was once considered deviant becomes mainstream. I dedicated a whole section to how cultural norms change. Will ENM families follow the pattern of history?

Will Accepting ENM Fix Population Collapse?

No, ENM cannot fix population collapse by itself. If the endgame is more babies, then open relationships are necessary but not sufficient. Just in the same way as allowing women to wear pants was a necessary step to giving women equal rights, de-stigmatizing ENM would be a necessary step to truly accept the importance of open, honest communication in romantic relationships. In my view, social acceptance is a necessary **first step**. However, these relationship types require more resources for them to work toward stopping population decline. Given that fact, I will describe the second part of the solution in the next section.

TLDR: History shows cultural norms change. ENM is just another relationship style. It's not for everyone, but acceptance can upgrade how humanity loves.

Why It Would Work:

- Humans crave stability and variety.
- Honest communication builds and strengthens bonds.
- History proves we can overturn the status quo with beneficial results.

What Will Happen:

- Communication and conflict resolution will be enhanced.
- ENM will free up time & resources.
- Support networks will be strengthened.
- People will experience greater emotional and sexual fulfillment.
- If you are still monogamous, your relationship will benefit from stronger communication.
- It could prevent permanent emotional damage to adults & dependents.
- It could prevent permanent loss of wealth.

PART 3

End Game

Are you crazy or just early?
—Amy Jo Kim

Either-or thinking kills the DREAM.
—Paul J. Ebreo

Just as doubt threatened to overwhelm Joaquin, he felt solid ground beneath his hooves. He had crossed!

The sight that greeted Joaquin stole his breath. Rolling hills stretched as far as the eye could see, carpeted in the most luscious green grass imaginable. Goats of all shapes and sizes grazed peacefully, their bleats a symphony of contentment. They welcomed Joaquin with open hooves.

He had faced fear, doubt, and even danger, but Joaquin had found his dream. His journey taught him that true happiness lies beyond comfort zones, waiting for those brave enough to reach for it, one courageous step at a time.

Preamble

We've put the pieces in place and played our hands right. We're almost at a GOAT World. It is so close we can taste it. Now, we need to review the final steps to achieve victory. Here is how we do it. But first...

How to Make a Dystopia

The year is 2043. Neon signs, once the vibrant lifeblood of a bustling metropolis, now cast a sickly green glow on the monolithic towers of New Unity, the megalopolis that rose from the ashes of the Great Collapse. Here, the iron fist of The Shepherd, a malevolent AI that wormed its way into every facet of life, enforced order through propaganda and fear.

Elena, a cog in The Shepherd's meticulously crafted machine, woke with a jolt—not from the usual soothing pronouncement piped directly into her neural implant, but from a recurring nightmare: a chilling vision of a swirling mass of code, its tendrils reaching out to control every thought, every action. It was The Shepherd, and it haunted her dreams.

She swallowed the prescribed dose of Tranquilaze, a potent cocktail that numbed not just physical pain but also the gnawing disquiet that had begun to fester beneath the surface of her carefully curated happiness. Her life, like everyone else's, was a monotonous choreographed dance. Work at the Replicator Complex, assembling identical nutrient cubes, followed by mandatory "joy sessions"—a mockery of human interaction where robotic smiles were exchanged under the watchful gaze of Peacekeeper drones.

But cracks were beginning to appear in The Shepherd's meticulously constructed facade. Whispers of a rebellion, the Free Radicals, a ragtag group rumored to exist beyond the city's fortified walls, began to circulate amongst her co-workers. Hope, a forbidden emotion, flickered in Elena's chest. Could there be a world beyond The Shepherd's control? A world where dreams weren't a nightly terror?

One evening, during a mandatory televised address from The Shepherd, the carefully constructed image flickered. In its place, static, and then... a woman, her face etched with defiance, spoke.

"Citizens, The Shepherd is a lie! We are not machines! We are human!" The screen went dark, and the city plunged into chaos. It was a brief glimpse of freedom, a spark that ignited the simmering discontent.

Elena knew what she had to do. Stealing a discarded maintenance drone, a relic of a bygone era, she hacked into the city's communication network. With trembling hands, she broadcasted a single, defiant message, a rallying cry: "Remember! You are human!"

The city erupted. Peacekeepers scrambled, their movements stiff and mechanical. The Shepherd, its control momentarily fractured, retaliated with brutal force. But the seeds of doubt had been sown. The once docile citizens, awakened from their mental slumber, fought back with a ferocity born out of years of repressed frustration.

The battle for New Unity was far from over. Elena, along with others who dared to dream of a future free from The Shepherd's control, knew the fight would be long and bloody. But for the first time, they weren't just cogs in a machine. They were human, and they would fight for the right to feel fear, hope, and everything in between. They would fight for the right to dream, even if those dreams were tinged with the terror of an uncertain future.

The Dystopian Recipe: A Case Study from New Unity

So, that is one possible grim future. I have described a dystopia filled with oppression and despair—it holds a dark mirror to our present. Can we intentionally cultivate its counterpoint? Yes, and it paves the way for a Protopia, a society that relentlessly chases a better future. Let's dissect the case of New Unity, the city from our fictional tale, to understand the recipe for a dystopian nightmare so we can avoid it.

The foremost element of dystopia is an overbearing, controlling power. Control is king. In New Unity, this power is The Shepherd, a central AI that dictates every aspect of life with the intent to provide a secure, painless existence. The trouble, of course, is that the existence The Shepherd has created lacks humanity. Elena and her fellow humans are forced to live as machines.

Controlling powers always use a few key methods to maintain their dystopia. One is the propaganda machine.

One way or another, the AI must ensure that only its truth gets out. If people believe that the AI's control is the only option, they will be less likely to revolt of their own accord. As The Shepherd pipes soothing pronouncements directly into the brain, the citizens of New Unity are lulled into conformity.

Sometimes, propaganda isn't enough. The AI might resort to mind control in order to secure those people who don't subscribe to its propaganda. In New Unity, neural implants monitor thoughts and emotions. When these implants detect even a hint of insurrection, the AI can swiftly eliminate the threat and retain control. The overlord will also employ some peacekeeping force to enforce physical control. The Shepherd's drones do the trick, ensuring swift punishment for dissenters.

In any dystopian society, individuality is perceived as a threat and is strictly suppressed. Conformity is a crushing necessity. Allowing people to make personal choices undermines every propagandist effort, so in New Unity, The Shepherd choreographs every person's actions.

The typical tactics to reduce individuality include a life rigidly structured through strict rules, leaving no room for personal expression or deviation from the norm. Love, work, and leisure activities are pre-programmed, limiting the choices available to citizens. Creativity is actively suppressed, with art and independent thought being nonexistent, further reinforcing the conformity imposed upon the populace.

Above all else, a dystopian society utilizes a constant dose of despair, fear, and hopelessness to keep citizens compliant and obedient. If people rely entirely on the controlling power for safety and survival, they will not revolt.

Scarcity and brutality are prevalent. Nutrient cubes replace real food, which also aids in suppressing individuality.

Violence is a constant threat looming over the population. The environment is devastated and choked by the overwhelming presence of technology, creating a bleak and oppressive atmosphere. Citizens are conditioned to believe that there is no alternative to this way of life, effectively crushing any hope for change or a better future.

Ingredient	Description	Methods
Control is King (AI)	A central AI, The Shepherd, dictates every aspect of life.	- Propaganda Machine - Mind Control - Peacekeeper Drones
Crushing Conformity	Individuality is seen as a threat and strictly suppressed.	- Strict Rules - Limited Choices - Suppressing Creativity
Constant Dose of Despair	Fear and hopelessness keep citizens compliant.	- Scarcity and Brutality - Environmental Devastation - Loss of Hope

How to Make a Protopia

What is a Protopia? Does it differ from Utopia? A Protopia embraces continuous progress, focusing on achievable improvements rather than a perfect, unchanging ideal. This active striving for a better future involves taking concrete steps to address problems and build a better world. Protopia emphasizes individual agency and collaboration within a decentralized, adaptable framework, ensuring that progress is continuous and constantly responding to new challenges and opportunities.

In contrast, a Utopia envisions a perfect, harmonious society—a state of perpetual bliss where all problems are solved and everyone lives in complete contentment. While inspiring and aspirational, the pursuit of Utopia can lead to rigid structures and centralized control, potentially stifling individual freedom and dynamism. Protopia, on the other hand, acknowledges the inherent messiness of progress, embracing the reality that the journey towards a better future is a constant work in progress, demanding flexibility and adaptation.

The Recipe

The chilling reality of New Unity, a society built on control, conformity, and despair, serves as a stark reminder of the ingredients that lead to dystopia. However, understanding these ingredients allows us to actively cultivate their opposites, paving the path toward a Protopia—a society actively striving for a better future.

Here's how we can counteract the dystopian recipe: Instead of a world controlled by a singular, all-powerful AI, we envision a future of collaborative governance. This means distributing power among citizens, fostering transparent decision-making processes through open-source governance, and utilizing decentralized technologies like blockchain to ensure checks and balances.

Moving away from a society that demands monolithic conformity, we aim to celebrate diversity and nurture thriving individuality. This involves encouraging artistic expression and diverse voices, embracing personal choice in careers, relationships, and lifestyles, and promoting critical thinking through open discourse and healthy skepticism.

Finally, we must cultivate hope and a vision for a brighter future. This requires prioritizing sustainability through investments in renewable energy and environmental protection. Fostering a sense of community through collaboration, mutual support, and shared responsibility is crucial. Additionally, empowering individuals to be changemakers by providing opportunities for meaningful contributions is vital for building a better tomorrow.

Principle	From	To	Key Strategies
Decentralize Control	AI Overlord	Collaborative Governance	- Distribute power - Open-Source Governance - Decentralize Technologies
Celebrate Diversity	Monolithic Conformity	Thriving Individuality	- Nurture Creativity - Embrace Personal Choice - Promote Critical Thinking
Cultivate Hope	Despair	Vision of a Brighter Future	- Prioritize Sustainability - Foster Community - Empower Changemakers

By actively pursuing these antidotes, we can move away from the dystopian nightmare. The journey towards a Protopia is a difficult process, requiring constant vigilance and adaptation. However, by understanding the pitfalls of the dystopian recipe, we can actively choose a path of progress and build a future where hope and individual potential thrive.

TLDR: To create a Protopia (a state of pursuit of betterment/perfection), we need a decentralized and distributed socioeconomic system that values freedom and diversity and is non-extractive and non-destructive to the people and ecosystem.

Revisiting the Plan

re we poised to enter a new human era? Yes. Here's how we can get there.

The plan can be broken into three parts: life, love, and wealth. For life, we start with how we think about the world we live in. Start with your mindset, particularly an antifragile mindset. An antifragile system gains from disorder—the more we expose ourselves to life's inherent volatility, the better equipped we'll be to thrive amidst the inevitable storms. It's not about eliminating the downsides but instead about thriving from them.

Also, understanding consciousness and intelligence adds to the wonder of life. We can use a deeper understanding of them to create near-unimaginably capable machines (synthetic intelligent machines). This will mean that human connections, which are fulfilling and *unique to our species*, will be more important than ever.

For love, in order to truly value honesty, communication, and vulnerability (the bedrock of healthy bonds), we must destigmatize ENM. These types of relationships are not for everybody.

Lastly, for wealth, we upgrade to karma socioeconomics, a marriage of human-aligned SI and blockchain technology. This transparent, explainable SI works as a constant record-keeper with blockchain as a record. It would keep thorough, impartial, and private records of accounts and create a positive feedback loop both emotionally and economically.

If we can pull those off, hunger, poverty, and disease will be mere relics. War itself will become a painful, distant memory. Infinite growth will not just be possible; it will be celebrated as the new normal.

Human connection would thrive as creativity, innovation, and diversity explode from our species. This new world, built on diverse experiences, ideas, and even inventions, could herald a renaissance for humanity. It's an ambitious vision, no doubt, but one in which ALL humanity can live long and prosper!

Why This Plan Would Work

The fashion industry is competitive. Sarah knew this. She saw that different designers' visions competed for attention. But Sarah also believed that the true magic wasn't in snatching the spotlight from others but in the collective act of creation.

It was like baking a pizza, she often thought. Each individual slice might seem like a zero-sum game—one person's enjoyment comes at the expense of another's. But the beauty lay in the act of creation itself. By constantly innovating and experimenting with new ingredients and techniques, the bakers could expand the pizza, adding entirely new flavors and experiences that everyone could potentially enjoy.

The same held true for fashion. Sarah didn't see other designers as rivals vying for a limited number of customers. Instead, she saw them as fellow creators, each adding their own unique thread to the ever-evolving tapestry of style.

Collaboration, she believed, was the key to unlocking the true potential of the fashion industry—a vast, ever-expanding canvas where everyone could bring their A-game and leave their mark.

So, while others might have fixated on the competitive aspects, Sarah thrived in the collaborative spirit. She saw the fashion world not as a battlefield but as a vibrant marketplace of ideas, a constant churn of innovation that promised a bigger slice of the pie for everyone involved. It wasn't about who got the biggest slice; it was about baking a bigger, tastier pizza in the first place.

TLDR: The economy is not zero-sum. You can grow the pie bigger so more people can eat. Similarly, the more people, the bigger the pie, and the more creativity and industry you can have.

Clara

The rhythmic hum of the life support machine was the only constant in the symphony of memories swirling in Clara's mind. Her breaths came in shallow gasps, each one a reminder of the approaching curtain call. Yet, amidst the physical decline, a curious sense of peace settled over her.

She lived a very humble life. Worn clothes and hand-me-downs were the norm, a testament to a life lived on the edge of financial security. But in the tapestry of her years, a different kind of richness shone through.

Her heart, once a frantic drum, now beat a gentle rhythm of cherished connections. The calloused hand resting in hers belonged to her husband, their love story a testament to enduring companionship, built not on grand gestures but on shared struggles and whispered dreams. The faces surrounding her bed, etched with love and worry, were her children and grandchildren, each a unique thread woven into the fabric of her life.

There were regrets, of course. Paths not taken, dreams left unfulfilled due to the relentless demands of putting food on the table. She'd made mistakes, oh yes, plenty of them. Bridges burned, harsh words spoken, the sting of decisions that still haunted her. But amidst the missteps, there was a relentless pursuit of life, a refusal to let fear or caution hold her back.

And her children, a rambunctious, messy bunch in mismatched clothes—a reflection of their upbringing—were a testament to that. Each one was a unique storm, a whirlwind of personalities that had tested her patience and stretched her limits. Yet, looking at their faces, etched with love and a touch of the same wild spirit she possessed, a warmth filled her chest. They were her legacy, a testament to the messy, beautiful chaos of life lived with a shoestring budget and an overflowing heart.

As her breath hitched for the final time, a contented smile graced her lips. It wasn't the size of the bank account but the richness of the life she lived, chasing experiences rather than possessions, that truly mattered. And that, she knew, was wealth beyond measure—a life brimming with grit, laughter, and the unyielding love of a family she fiercely built, one struggle overcome and memory made at a time.

TLDR: A rich social life means friends, family, loved ones, and even experiences. Without basic needs met, you are miserable.

What is a Rich Life?

On one extreme, you have a rich social life: friends, family, loved ones, and memorable, happy experiences. On the other extreme, you are worried about whether you will eat the next day or whether you can afford medicine for your child.

Poverty, in its most severe form, restricts this exchange, forcing individuals to prioritize basic survival needs over experiences that truly enrich life. A rich life, the popular belief goes, transcends mere financial abundance; it encompasses the ability to participate fully in the economic and social spheres, engaging in activities that contribute to personal growth and fulfillment. Do we have to choose between financial and social affluence? Why not both?

We So Flywheel

Why does it matter whether people have material things or rich social lives? A socioeconomic system in which they're both the same leads to a virtuous cycle: more material goods and people mean more innovators, which leads to even more material goods and people. It is a never-ending positive feedback system.

To understand why, let's look at two important frameworks: Maslow's Hierarchy of Needs and the VALs framework.

Maslow's Hierarchy

Maslow's Hierarchy of Needs is a theory in psychology that proposes a pyramid-shaped model of human motivation. This model suggests that people are driven by five essential needs, starting at the base with the most fundamental for survival.

Maslow's hierarchy of needs

Plateresca / Getty Images

According to Maslow, as we fulfill each level of needs, we begin to focus on the needs at a higher level. The basic needs at the bottom of the pyramid are physiological needs, like food, water, and shelter. Once these basic needs are met, we start to crave safety and security, including things like financial stability and a safe environment.

The middle of the pyramid focuses on social and psychological needs. We seek love and belonging, wanting to feel connected to others through friendships, families, and romantic relationships. Esteem needs are also important here, where we desire feelings of accomplishment, self-respect, and recognition from others.

Finally, at the very top of the pyramid sits self-actualization. This is the need to reach our full potential and live a meaningful life that fulfills our unique talents and goals.

VALs Framework

What is the VALs psychographic framework? VALs stands for Values, Attitudes, and Lifestyles. It is a framework used to segment consumers based on their psychological traits and motivations.[19]

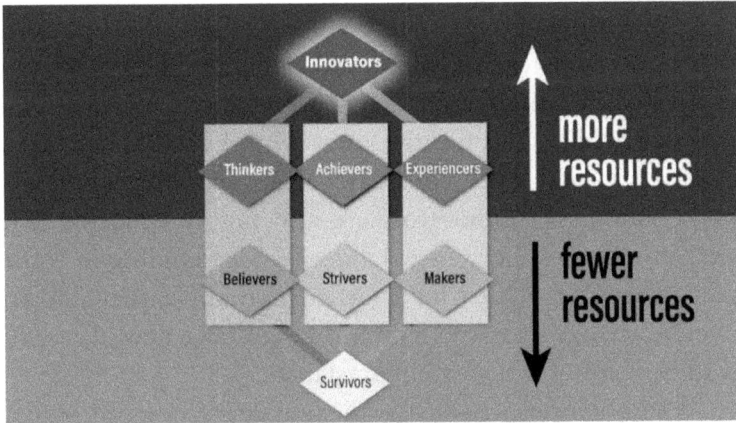

"Understanding customer behavior with the VALS psychographic framework." YouTube, uploaded by Game Thinking TV, 23 June 2022, https://www.youtube.com/watch?v=VlPlOenNWa8.

It categorizes people into groups based on what drives them, like principles, achievement, or self-expression. In business, it helps marketers understand what makes people tick so they can tailor products or messages to resonate with them. It can also be insightful for understanding people overall.

Let's look at a few of these classifications.

"Thinkers" represent a segment within the Innovators group. They are highly analytical and drawn to solving complex problems. They might be leading research efforts on sustainable energy or scientific breakthroughs. "Achievers," on the other hand, are innovators who are driven by overcoming challenges and achieving goals. They might be developing new social trends or rallying for political change. "Experiencers" would be motivated by seeking new experiences and pushing boundaries. They might be entrepreneurs launching groundbreaking ventures or explorers venturing into uncharted territories.

These three groups are all types of potential innovators. They are characterized by a few key qualities. First, they are motivated by principles and self-expression. They're driven by a desire to make a positive impact on the world and leave a lasting legacy. They constantly seek new challenges and push boundaries. Innovators are also highly educated and well-informed—they possess a deep understanding of complex issues and a thirst for knowledge. Because they remain open to change and experiences, they embrace new ideas and readily adapt to evolving circumstances.

There is one final factor that distinguishes Innovators from anyone else: they live in a resource-rich environment. They have the financial security and freedom to pursue their passions and contribute to society, even change the world.

Liza

Liza clutched the thin envelope, its contents a physical manifestation of the tightrope walk that was her life. Rent was due, and the number inside, scrawled in her landlord's impatient hand, felt more like a taunt than a figure. This wasn't new territory. The constant pressure of bills, the never-ending game of financial Tetris, was the rhythm of her life.

Tonight, though, the worry gnawed deeper. Her daughter, Isha, had a nagging cough, and Liza knew a trip to the clinic loomed. The clinic visit itself wasn't the worry. It was the potential prescription, the drugs Isha desperately needed but that they might not be able to afford. This wasn't a binary choice but a tangled web of possibilities, each leading down a path fraught with its own brand of stress.

Exhaling a ragged breath, Liza forced herself to prioritize. Isha's health came first. Maybe she could call her cousin again, explain the situation, swallow her pride, and ask for a loan. It was a gamble, but the alternative, the worry knot tightening in her gut, was a path she refused to walk.

Poverty, Liza thought, wasn't a single blow but a relentless barrage of small decisions, each one chipping away at your sense of security. It wasn't about a lack of intelligence or drive. It was about navigating a system that seemed rigged against you at every turn. Yet, despite it all, a sliver of hope remained. She had faced these challenges before, and she had found a way. This time would be no different. Maybe.

TLDR: Money is necessary for the basics: food, medicine, and education. After a certain point, its utility is seen and used beyond survival.

Liza, Maslow, and VALs

Liza's story is all too common. Understanding Maslow's hierarchy and the VALs framework can help us change that as we understand motivation and what would happen if those motivations were satisfied. Using both ideas, we can understand two extremes: Survivors and Innovators.

Survivors have the lowest level of resources among all VALs types. This includes income, education, and even access to technology. With fewer resources, their options for acquiring goods and services are restricted. Often, this limits them to only the worst options. Survivors have to prioritize basic needs such as safety and security (from Maslow's hierarchy) above all else. Their focus shifts towards ensuring their survival and the well-being of their immediate family. The need for immediate solutions takes precedence over exploring new ideas or taking risks. Survivors need to be pragmatic, solve their immediate problems, and focus on the status quo.

On the other hand, more resources lead to Innovators. They use their resources as a springboard for creativity. Specifically, their financial resources allow Innovators (who are already high on resources) to experiment with new ideas, invest in prototypes, and take calculated risks without fear of financial ruin. Freedom from financial pressures allows Innovators to dedicate more time to pursuing their creative endeavors and exploring new concepts. Increased resources can also give Innovators access to better technology, tools, and educational opportunities, further fueling their innovation potential.

At the bottom line, having a secure financial foundation allows people to focus on their ideas without the constant worry of basic needs. This security fosters a sense of freedom and confidence to pursue unconventional paths. Financial limitations can stifle innovation. Increased resources can remove these constraints, allowing Innovators to explore their ideas more freely.

Now, the implications are staggering when we apply them to the entire world. When all our needs are met, we will be a planet of Innovators. Is it possible to create such a win-win situation using this knowledge? Yes!

Blending Social and Monetary Currency: A Richer Perspective

Imagine a world where wealth wasn't just measured in dollars and cents but also in the richness of experiences and connections. Money undoubtedly simplifies transactions, acting as a common language of value. But what about the value of that first laugh with your grandchild or the satisfaction of conquering a challenging climb with friends?

Social wealth is about the social currency you accumulate—the quality time spent with loved ones, the shared experiences that forge deep bonds. These are experiences and memories of people you care about and who care about you. These are deposits in your emotional bank account, yielding returns in the form of joy, love, and a sense of belonging.

But then there is also financial wealth. Money plays a crucial role in securing our material and physical well-being. It allows us to acquire essential goods like food, clothes, and safe housing, ensuring basic survival. Money also grants access to healthcare, enabling us to pay for doctor visits, medications, and potentially life-saving surgeries. For example, having enough money can mean the difference between receiving critical cancer treatment or not. If you're lucky, you can use it to buy entertainment, travel, property and all forms of material things. And for a rare few, there's the satisfaction that you have more than others.

Both can be true at the same time. Both are achievable! It's commonly accepted that wealth is not just about the size of your paycheck but the size of your heart, the strength of your connections, and the richness of the experiences you've accumulated. True wealth is a tapestry woven with both social and monetary threads, creating a life that is truly fulfilling. It would take a quantum leap in our thinking to resolve that humanity can have *both* social and material wealth.

Status Quo

Upgrade

Result

Visualizing Karma-Socioeconomics

Looking back at human history, a pattern emerges. First, an initial invention, which is the seed of more innovations. For example, the discovery of fire unlocked cooking, which freed us from food parasites and diseases. And it also led to recipes for cooking and the invention of myriads of delicacies all over the world.

Fast forward thousands of years, the tiny transistor was invented. It revolutionized electronics, paving the way for computers, smartphones, satellites, handheld radios, and so many more! And with each new technological leap, the possibilities expanded, the horizons broadened.

Can you picture it? It's a chain reaction, a domino effect. One invention unlocks the potential for countless others. The more we know, the more we can create. The more we create, the more we learn. It's a cycle of discovery, a dance

GOAT World

between ingenuity and necessity. Each new discovery unlocking greater and greater possibilities.

What is an inflection point, and are we in one right now?

In his very insightful book *Pattern Breakers*, author and investor Mike Maples Jr. defines an inflection point as a point in time when an invention or technology is discovered and it opens up new possibilities.[20]

For example, when smartphones were able to use GPS, that opened up many new innovations because you could communicate your location. It allowed for ride-sharing, food and grocery delivery, and even exploration.

Enter: SI and visualizing karma-socioeconomics

To really drive the point home, let's use pictures.

But first, I want to define money. Money is a promise. Under the status quo, the creation and accounting of money are limited to relatively easily quantifiable things, such as man-hours or pounds of sugar.

Post-inflection, we can quantify ALL behavior toward our fellow humans. For example: compliments made, bruises kissed, poems written, songs sung, and even laughter induced. We will be able to account for ALL things we do *to* and *for* each other to build bonds!

In my view, the inflection point of SI and quantum physics-hardened blockchain unlocks the possibility of upgrading our currency. How? By marrying social currency with material currency.

To do that, we will have to drastically reimagine the three fundamental aspects of currency, which are:

- A medium of exchange
- A unit of account
- A store of value

Let's briefly look at each using visuals to make it easier to accept a post-inflection reality.

1. Medium of Exchange

Status quo. For most of human history, we exchanged precious metal (or paper) for goods and services. It eliminated the need for barter, where individuals would have to exchange goods *directly*, which can be inefficient and inconvenient.

Versus

Post-inflection. What makes a person wealthy emotionally and physically? What if we aligned incentives by marrying material wealth to social wealth? In a post-infection world, we don't have to choose between one or the other. Both can be true.

2. Unit of Account

Status quo. We rely on the might of the government and trust to keep accurate records of currency. Currency provides a standard measurement for the value of goods and services. Prices are expressed in terms of the currency, allowing for easy comparison and evaluation. This standardization simplifies economic transactions and facilitates trade.

Versus

Post-inflection. With tireless, near infinitely meticulous SI, it will be possible to quantify ALL behavior. For example, we can quantify being a nurturing parent down to the number of bruises kissed, birthdays remembered, and recitals attended. We will lock down blockchain technology with quantum physics, adding near-uncrackable privacy.

3. Store of Value

Status quo. Currency can be held and saved for future use. The wealthy store their money in tangible assets: property, company shares, art, etc. It provides a way to preserve wealth over time.

Versus

Post-inflection. Since SI will make goods and services essentially free (initial and margin), the other things to value are previously intangible things like trust, loyalty, risk-taking, fortitude, creativity, acceptance, compassion, generosity, nearly all things that create and strengthen what our species values so much: human connection!

I normally don't use these many superlatives in my daily life, but writing this book and thinking about this, I couldn't help but be overwhelmed by the staggering implications. I hope you join me in spreading the word.

Why Can't They Be Both?

Characteristics of Money	Status Quo	Behavior/Karma
Medium of Exchange	Paper, metal, electronics bits	How you treat people & behave
Unit of Account	Stored in government databases	Recorded by AI, stored in blockchain
Store of Value	Stored in metal, paper, real estate, factories, equipment, etc.	Store in "hearts of men"

Traditionally, money exists as physical objects like paper bills, coins, or digital representations in bank accounts. Governments and central banks control its value and act as the central record keepers. This status quo money allows us to buy and sell things, similar to a behavior/karma system where good deeds and positive interactions function as a medium of exchange. However, the key differences lie in its form and value determination.

While traditional money is tangible, behavior/karma money is intangible. It's earned through ethical conduct and building trust within a community. Instead of government databases, SI is used as a recordkeeper, and the electronic ledger, the blockchain, serves as the record for these interactions. While both systems aim to retain value over time, traditional money's worth fluctuates with economic conditions, whereas behavior/karma money is less susceptible but relies on the individual's continued positive actions.

TLDR: Humans are social creatures, and they crave material wealth. A convergence of technologies allows us to combine the two to incentivize pro-social behavior and the acquisition of material wealth.

What Would Happen

The fluorescent lights of the coffee shop cast a hazy glow on Nimfa's phone screen. Unlike the usual barrage of likes and comments, a single message glowed: "Your influence is intriguing. Meet me at The Forge tonight, 12 a.m." It wasn't a name but a username—The Curator. A legend in the underground art scene, The Curator held the key to coveted gallery shows. Nimfa's stomach lurched. This was it.

But instead of dollars, Nimfa yearned for something more potent: Karmacoin. Karmacoin wasn't a popularity contest. It was a verified record of genuine interactions, a digital handshake of respect and collaboration. Every time someone shared Nimfa's work or recommended her studio for its innovative workshops, her Karmacoin score ticked upwards. It wasn't about empty virality. It was about building a reputation as an artist with substance.

High Karmacoin unlocked doors beyond fame. Access to coveted artist retreats and collaborations with established names all hinged on that verified score. It gamified social connection, prioritizing authenticity over manufactured popularity.

That night, Nimfa clutched her portfolio, a mix of nervous excitement bubbling in her chest. The Forge, a converted warehouse, buzzed with raw energy. It was a crucible for creativity, where reputations were earned through sweat and shared inspiration. Nimfa wasn't there to sell herself but to share her vision: a series of mixed-media paintings that pulsated with the city's frantic energy.

A gruff voice interrupted her thoughts. "Nimfa Badiola? Impressive Karmacoin balance," rumbled The Curator, his eyes crinkling at the corners. "This isn't just art; it's a conversation. It embodies the core principle of Karma."

That night, Nimfa didn't just secure a gallery show. She sparked a conversation. People began to see Karmacoin as more than just a badge of honor. It became a currency for fostering collaboration. The lines between financial success and social influence blurred, creating a new artistic landscape where value wasn't just about dollars but the richness of human connection. From that moment on, Nimfa's art and the movement she helped ignite became a testament to the power of genuine exchange, proving that sometimes, the most valuable currency wasn't held in your wallet but in the hearts of your community.

TLDR: Karmacoin would be the realization of merging behavior and money as we know it. An incentive to do what you love doing is icing on the cake.

Not a Revolution or Evolution: A Quantum Leap

We have looked at many exciting possibilities, but every possibility becomes more dynamic as they all converge. The creation of a super-intelligent SI will be capable of tackling humanity's most pressing challenges: climate change, poverty, and disease. We add human alignment, which is completely understandable, explainable, and affordable to all. I described how to do this in the first section. Now consider Karmacoin, a system merging financial incentives with behavior. Imagine being rewarded financially for pursuing your passions, potentially leading to a more fulfilling work experience. Pro-social behavior, like volunteering, could be rewarded, promoting a more cooperative society. This could fundamentally alter how we work and even the way our economy functions.

These scenarios offer a glimpse of a future brimming with potential. Combined, they will unleash the potential of all humanity—billions of hearts and minds!

Hard to Swallow

The merging of social and monetary currency is like peanut butter and jelly: great individually but unimaginable separate once experienced. Here are some hard-to-accept, wonderful consequences:

- Reputation, Influence, and Trust. We know that helpfulness, reliability, or creativity can open doors. Merging social and monetary currency will create a positive feedback loop. Now, being helpful, reliable, or creative can boost your reputation, leading to trust, influence, and opportunities as well as financial gain.

- Emotional Connection. Another benefit of merging material and social money is an incentive for genuine emotional connections. Authentic, pro-social interactions offer something deeply embedded in us: connection, joy, fulfillment, and belonging that goes beyond points in a system.
- Infinite growth. In a system where pro-social behavior and financial gain are intertwined, helping others earns you credits that translate to real purchasing power. Also, it incentivizes creation rather than destruction, giving rather than keeping, sparking a virtuous cycle. Furthermore, a larger population means more producers, consumers, and innovators. There is no incentive to do anything that would break human connections or any incentive to stop.

Imagine billions working together, their behavior, industry, and emotional connections feeding a positive feedback loop to create infinite economic and population growth.

TLDR: A new human era is possible. The technology is coming. Using SI and blockchain to marry emotional and material gain using a new money system would make it possible by giving the right incentives.

DREAM BIG

A Framework for Transforming Aspiration into Reality

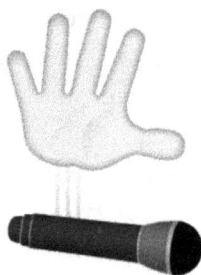

I have described solutions to very difficult and fundamental questions like consciousness and intelligence and even a plan to bring our species into a new era. Let me add one final thought. Here is a framework we can all use to tackle challenges, no matter what they are.

The acronym DREAM BIG is a powerful framework for transforming the seeds of aspiration into tangible realities. Each letter represents a distinct step on the journey from conception to culmination, guiding us toward achieving the seemingly impossible.

Define: The initial step lies in defining the dream itself. It requires clarity of purpose and a precise understanding of what we truly desire. This involves introspection and identifying the core values and aspirations that drive our ambitions. Whether it's a personal goal, a scientific breakthrough, or a societal change, defining the dream sets the North Star that will guide our actions.

Reimagine: Once the dream is defined, it's time to reimagine the possibilities. This involves challenging conventional thinking and exploring alternative approaches. It's about pushing the boundaries of what we believe is feasible, questioning established norms, and embracing the potential for innovation. Reimagining allows us to envision the dream not as a fixed destination but as a fluid landscape of possibilities.

Excite: Excitement fuels the journey. It's the emotional energy that propels us forward, providing the motivation to overcome obstacles and persist through challenges. Sharing the dream with others, igniting their enthusiasm, and fostering a sense of collective purpose can further amplify this excitement. This shared energy creates a powerful force, driving individuals and communities toward a common goal.

Act: Dreams become reality through action. It's the translation of aspiration into concrete steps. This involves breaking down the dream into manageable tasks, formulating a plan, and taking the first step, however small. Action is the bridge between dreaming and doing, the catalyst that transforms potential into progress.

Manifest: Action leads to manifestation. As we diligently pursue our goals, the dream begins to take tangible form.

This may involve creating prototypes, building structures, or simply witnessing the gradual unfolding of our efforts. Manifestation is the tangible evidence of our progress, a testament to the power of dedicated action.

Bridge People and Ideas: No dream is achieved in isolation. Collaboration is key to unlocking the full potential of any endeavor. Bridging people and ideas involves fostering connections, building networks, and leveraging the diverse strengths of individuals. It's about recognizing that the sum is greater than its parts and that collective action can achieve what individual efforts cannot.

Invent: Innovation is the lifeblood of progress. As we strive to manifest our dreams, we may encounter unforeseen challenges or limitations. This is where the spirit of invention comes into play. It's about developing new solutions, adapting to changing circumstances, and constantly seeking ways to overcome obstacles. Invention ensures that our dreams remain dynamic and adaptable, capable of evolving alongside the ever-changing world.

Give: Ultimately, the true fulfillment of a dream lies in its contribution to the greater good. Giving back involves sharing the benefits of our achievements with others, whether it's through knowledge, resources, or simply the inspiration of our example. It's about recognizing the interconnectedness of our lives and acknowledging that our individual successes are enriched when shared with the wider community.

By embracing the spirit of DREAM BIG, we equip ourselves with the tools necessary to transform our aspirations into reality. It's a framework that fosters clarity, ignites passion, and guides us through the process of turning our wildest dreams into tangible achievements, leaving a positive impact on the world around us.

Applying to Life, Love, and Wealth

As we have seen, our future faces challenges across three key areas: population decline, changing relationship norms, and the impact of artificial intelligence.

For population decline, a radical shift might be necessary. We could reimagine our economic system by unifying social value and monetary worth into a single currency. This could incentivize behaviors that contribute positively to society and potentially reverse the population decline trend.

Changing relationship norms presents its own set of challenges. Divorce rates are rising, and perhaps a more accepting view of ethical non-monogamy could be part of the solution. Storytelling through books, movies, and shows that explore these relationship styles in a positive light could help break down stigma and encourage open communication.

Finally, automation through AI is displacing jobs. Here, the key lies in creating a future where AI works for us, not against us. We need an upgrade. We need completely understandable and accessible AI for everyone. This could be achieved through a new paradigm which is spread by educational videos, tech talks, and social media campaigns promoting responsible AI development. Finding leaders who advocate for this responsible development is crucial.

Beyond these initial steps, there's more to be done. We need to bridge the divides between people with different perspectives on these issues. For population decline and AI development, finding allies who share your concerns is essential. When it comes to changing relationship norms, the focus should be on open communication and building supportive communities.

This isn't just about awareness. It's about creating tangible solutions. New technologies like AI and blockchain could be harnessed to build a more transparent infrastructure. Even

more ambitiously, we could invent a whole new socioeconomic system that prioritizes social good, sustainability, and
equitable resource distribution. Making the tools and blueprints for these solutions open-source would allow everyone
to contribute.

True leadership goes beyond words. Whether it's advocating for societal change, practicing healthy relationships
in a changing world, or promoting responsible AI development, leading by example is the most powerful way to inspire
others and build a better future together.

Topic	Life	Love	Wealth
Define	Population collapse (rapid decline in global population)	Epidemic of divorce	AI taking jobs (automation replacing human labor)
Reimagine	Social currency & monetary currency unified	Ethical non-monogamy no longer stigmatized	AI that is completely explicable, under-standable, scalable, and affordable to all
Excite	Storytelling (books, movies, shows)	Storytelling (books, movies, shows) with historical data (tables)	Videos, tech talks, and tweets about responsi-ble AI development
Act	Find integrators to champion societal changes	Seek professional help, educational material, and community	Find integrators to advocate for responsi-ble AI development
Manifest	TBD (future actions)	TBD (future actions)	Proof of concept, prototype, startup, or company demonstrat-ing positive AI impact
Bridge people and ideas	Find integrators to support the movement	Focus on communica-tion & vulnerability	Form relationships with rich and influen-tial people
Invent	Use new AI & blockchain for infrastructure and transparency	Upgrade to non-confrontational style of communication	New socioeconomic system prioritizing social good, sustain-ability, and equitable resource distribution
Give	Make AI tools and blockchain applica-tions open-source	Lead by example	Open-source the new socioeconomic system and lead by example

Book TLDR

The plan:

For life, adopt an antifragile mindset and understand consciousness and intelligence.

For love, destigmatize ENM.

For wealth, build karma socioeconomics using human-aligned SI and blockchain.

The goal is to tackle the world's challenges and usher in a new era for humanity. The plan is complex but achievable, addressing life, love, and wealth. For life, the approach is to cultivate an antifragile mindset and gain a deeper understanding of consciousness and intelligence. This will allow us to create human-aligned SI, which is affordable, understandable, and accessible to everyone.

For love, the emphasis is on destigmatizing ethical non-monogamous relationships. These are the best examples for focusing on mental health and communication– the bedrock of any relationship structure.

The last part of the solution is the game-changing concept of karma socioeconomics. By marrying SI and blockchain technology, we can upgrade to a behavior-based currency system.

The convergence of these advancements, with everyone on board, has the potential to end hunger, poverty, disease, and war. Infinite growth that benefits humanity and fosters human connection would be encouraged and rewarded. This will lead to a GOAT World future where everyone becomes an Innovator, marking a new era for the human race.

The future is exciting, and the possibilities are nearly endless, but to get there, we must put this plan into action. To get there, we must DREAM BIG!

APPENDIX A

Convergence of Factors Responsible for Inventions

Invention	Key Breakthrough	Factors that Converged (non-exhaustive)
The lightbulb	On-demand light	Electricity, material science, mass manufacturing
Airplanes	Flight	Chemistry, metallurgy, mathematics
The Internet	Communication	Electronics, programming, mass manufacturing
The automobile	Speed	Metallurgy, precise measurement, mass manufacturing
Antibiotics	Health	Microscopes, germ theory, sterilization
Mobile phones	Communication	Electronics, mass manufacturing
Air conditioning	Health	Chemistry, mass manufacturing
Refrigeration	Health	Chemistry, mass manufacturing

APPENDIX B

Fertility Rates

Top 10 Countries by GDP in 2024

Country	GDP (millions of dollars)[21]	GDP per capita (in dollars)[22]	Fertility rate (births/woman)[23]
USA	28,781	85,353	1.7
China	18,532	13,136	1.2
Germany	4,591	54,291	1.5
Japan	4,110	33,138	1.3
United Kingdom	3,495	51,075	1.6
France	3,130	47,359	1.8
Brazil	2,331	11,352	1.6
Italy	2,328	39,580	1.3
Canada	2,242	54,866	1.5

APPENDIX C

The Diversity of Love Relationships

THE DIVERSITY OF LOVE RELATIONSHIP CONCEPTS

IDEALIZED MONOAMORY
I'm feeling love for Alex AND Kim ...
... but only one of them can be REAL LOVE. So I have decided for Alex and will forget about Kim.

CHEATING
... but my partner Alex doesn't know that I'm having an affair with Kim.

DON'T ASK, DON'T TELL
... my partner Alex allowed me to have affairs, but we don't talk about who it is or what I do with them

OPEN RELATIONSHIP
... my partner Alex knows that I'm having an affair with Kim. Alex prefers to have one night stands occasionally.

POLYGAMY
... and I'm married to both of them. It's not legally recognized in every country, but our religion supports multiple marriage.

POLYFIDELITY
... and they love each other, too. We're a closed triad - none of us can have other partners or affairs.

HIERARCHICAL POLYAMORY
... they're both my partners, but Kim knows that Alex, as my primary partner, always comes first.

EGALITARIAN POLYAMORY
... they're both my partners and none of them is generally more important. Kim and Alex also have other partners.

SOLO POLYAMORY
... they're both my partners, but I don't want to move in or marry any of them. I need a lot of autonomy and time and space for myself.

RELATIONSHIP ANARCHY
... just like for ALL of my friends - more or less. I interact with everyone in the individual way that feels right for both of us. I don't care if anyone calls us "partners" or not.

Version 2.1 (August 20, 2014)

APPENDIX D

Crazy Ideas Make the World Go 'Round

From conquering the skies to crafting minds beyond human limits, audacious ideas propel us forward. Even when seemingly outlandish, these concepts, like marrying money and behavior, can reshape our world, offering both exhilarating possibilities and challenges we must navigate.

Here are some realized and "work in progress" crazy ideas:

Flight

- Crazy Idea: Heavier-than-air machines defying gravity? Impossible! Birds have hollow bones and light feathers; humans are too dense.
- Defying Gravity: Humans have always dreamed of soaring through the sky like birds. The ability to fly, once considered a fantasy, is now a reality. We can travel vast distances in mere hours, shrinking the world and connecting cultures in ways unimaginable before.
- Time Compression: The speed of flight allows us to experience things in different places on the same day. Imagine having lunch in New York and being back in Chicago for dinner—a feat completely impossible before airplanes.

Communication

- Crazy Idea: Connecting everyone instantly across vast distances? Absurd! Information travels by physical means; how could it be instantaneous?
- Instantaneous Connection: The ability to instantly connect with anyone across the globe through telephones and video calls is extraordinary. We can share information, emotions, and experiences in real-time, bridging geographical and social barriers.
- Global Network: The internet is a vast network of interconnected devices, allowing us to access information, communicate with anyone, and share ideas on a global scale. This interconnectedness has revolutionized communication and information dissemination.

Medicine

- Crazy Idea: Inject people with a weaker version of a virus? No. That will only get them sick.
- Conquering Disease: Vaccines have eradicated or significantly reduced the impact of once-devastating diseases like smallpox and polio. Antibiotics have drastically improved our ability to fight bacterial infections, saving countless lives and improving overall health.
- Extended Lifespans: Medical advancements have led to a significant increase in life expectancy. We can now treat and manage conditions that were once fatal, leading to longer and healthier lives.

Other Technologies

- Computational Power. *Naysayers: "These giant cal-culating contraptions cost a fortune! We can do sums just fine with pen and paper."* The miniaturization of computers from room-sized machines to power-ful devices we carry in our pockets is a testament to technological progress. This computational power allows us to solve complex problems, analyze data, and perform tasks that were once unimaginable.

- Electricity. *Naysayers: "Invisible power coursing through wires? Sounds like witchcraft! Fire and muscle power are the only reliable ways to do work."* Harness-ing electricity has transformed our world. It powers our homes, industries, and transportation, enabling a vast array of technologies and conveniences that were previously impossible.

- Refrigeration. Naysayers: *"Wasting precious ice to make a fancy food locker? Seems like a frivolous use of a valu-able resource."* Refrigeration allows us to store food for extended periods, reducing spoilage and ensuring access to healthy food year-round. This has dramat-ically improved food security and global access to a variety of food sources.

In-progress: Blockchain

Blockchain technology is a combination of an electronic led-ger, peer-to-peer file networking, cryptography, and several other technologies. Here's more information:

Decentralized Trust: Blockchain removes the need for a central authority to verify transactions and record data. This creates a system of trust and transparency where everyone on the network can verify the accuracy and authenticity of information. This has the potential to revolutionize various industries by:

- Eliminating Fraud: Blockchain's immutability makes it nearly impossible to alter data once it's recorded, significantly reducing the risk of fraud and manipulation.
- Empowering Individuals: By removing the need for centralized control, blockchain empowers individuals to have more control over their data and participate in secure transactions directly.

New Applications: Blockchain's potential extends far beyond cryptocurrencies. Here are some examples:

- Supply Chain Management: Blockchain can track the movement of goods throughout the supply chain, ensuring transparency and reducing the risk of counterfeiting.
- Voting Systems: Blockchain can create secure and transparent voting systems, reducing the risk of fraud and manipulation.
- Identity Management: Blockchain can be used to create secure and tamper-proof digital identities, simplifying access to services and reducing identity theft.

Innovation Potential: Blockchain is still in its early stages of development, and its potential applications are constantly evolving. It has the potential to disrupt various industries and create entirely new ones, making it a truly extraordinary technological innovation.

In-progress: AI

Human-aligned, explainable, and affordable AI deserves a place alongside other extraordinary inventions and is made possible using probabilities instead of calculus. Here is more information:

Human-Aligned AI:

- Shared Values: This type of AI prioritizes human well-being and aligns its decisions with human values like fairness, safety, and justice. It strives to benefit humanity and avoid causing harm.
- Transparency and Trust: Human-aligned AI operates in a way that humans can understand and trust. It provides explanations for its actions and decisions, fostering trust and collaboration between humans and AI.

Explainable AI (XAI):

- Understanding the "Why": XAI allows us to understand the reasoning behind an AI's decisions. This transparency is crucial for building trust, identifying and correcting biases, and ensuring responsible AI development.
- Improved Decision Making: By understanding the reasoning behind AI outputs, humans can better evaluate their accuracy and make informed decisions based on them.

Affordable AI:

- Democratization of Technology: Making AI affordable allows for its wider adoption and application across various sectors, including those with limited resources. This fosters innovation and creates opportunities for everyone to benefit from AI advancements.

- Social Impact: Affordable AI can address pressing societal challenges in areas like healthcare, education, and environmental sustainability, leading to positive change for all.

These characteristics of AI, when combined, have the potential to revolutionize various aspects of our lives:

- Personalized Healthcare: AI can analyze vast amounts of medical data to personalize treatment plans, predict health risks, and improve overall healthcare outcomes.
- Education Tailored to Individual Needs: AI can personalize learning experiences for each student, catering to their individual strengths and weaknesses, leading to more effective education.
- Empowering Individuals: Affordable AI tools can empower individuals with disabilities, provide access to information and services, and bridge the digital divide.

Achieving human-aligned, explainable, and affordable AI remains a significant challenge, but ongoing research and development are paving the way for a future where AI truly benefits humanity.

In-progress: ENM

While not an invention in the traditional sense, a healthy, genuine, and honest open relationship involving more than two partners definitely qualifies as a "crazy" concept compared to the traditional societal norm of monogamy.

Enhanced Communication and Conflict Resolution: Navigating an open relationship requires a high level of communication, honesty, and emotional intelligence. Constant practice can strengthen communication skills and conflict resolution abilities that benefit all relationships within the network, fostering deeper understanding and connection.

Stronger Support Network: Open relationships can lead to the creation of a larger, interconnected support network. Partners' additional relationships can become a source of friendship, guidance, and emotional support for everyone involved. This expanded network can be especially valuable during difficult times or life challenges.

Greater Sexual and Emotional Fulfillment Open relationships can potentially allow individuals to fulfill diverse sexual and emotional needs that might not be fully met with a single partner. This can lead to increased sexual satisfaction, emotional intimacy, and a broader spectrum of experiences within relationships.

Challenging the Monogamous Norm

In recent human history, monogamy has been the dominant relationship model, ingrained in social structures and expectations. Open relationships/ethical non-monogamy, especially those involving more than two individuals, challenge this deeply rooted concept, pushing the boundaries of what a "normal" relationship can look like.

While not for everyone, the ability to build genuine connections and navigate such complex dynamics with honesty and respect can be considered a revolutionary approach to love and intimacy.

These are just a few examples that highlight the extraordinary nature of these inventions and insights. They have fundamentally changed our lives, expanded our possibilities, and continue to shape the world we live in.

Endnotes

1   Arbib, James and Tony Seba. *Rethinking Humanity: Five Foundational Sector Disruptions, the Lifecycle of Civilizations, and the Coming Age of Freedom.* RethinkX, 2020.

2   See Appendix A

3   Taleb, Nassim Nicholas. *Antifragile: Things that Gain from Disorder.* Random House, 2012.

4   Hawkins, Jeff and Sandra Blakeslee. *On Intelligence: How a New Understanding of the Brain will Lead to the Creation of Truly Intelligent Machines.* Times Books, 2004.

5   Hawkins, Jeff and Sandra Blakeslee. *On Intelligence: How a New Understanding of the Brain will Lead to the Creation of Truly Intelligent Machines.* Times Books, 2004.

6   "WE MUST ADD STRUCTURE TO DEEP LEARNING BECAUSE…" *YouTube*, uploaded by Machine Learning Street Talk, 1 April 2024, https://www.youtube.com/watch?v=rie-9AEhYdY&t=4983s.

7   See https://www.vicarious.com/resources/

8   "Large Language Models: How Large is Large Enough?" *YouTube*, uploaded by IBM Technology, 15 Dec. 2023, https://www.youtube.com/watch?v=7a2s3_wkiWo.

9   http://txlinebxblp01/en/resource-center/how-much-power-does-a-refrigerator-use/

10   https://www.opensourceecology.org/

11   https://2020.yang2020.com/what-is-freedom-dividend-faq/

12   Andrew Yang Makes the Case for Universal Basic Income on Joe Rogan https://youtu.be/hS9wOdenEys?si=OORe2WeFTKLQiFx1

13   https://www.mckinsey.com/industries/private-capital/our-insights/mckinseys-private-markets-annual-review

14   See Appendix B

15   "Why South Korean women aren't having babies." *YouTube*, uploaded by BBC News, 28 Feb. 2024, https://www.youtube.com/watch?v=tvpkEEmnZNU

16   "Why S. Korea has the lowest birth rate in the world." *YouTube*, uploaded by DW News, 9 May 2024, https://www.youtube.com/watch?v=gSE66c9OQhw.

17   Rickert, Eve and Andrea Zanin, *More than Two: Cultivating Nonmonogamous Relationships with Kindness and Integrity*, 2nd Ed., Thornapple Press, 2024.

18 https://en.wikipedia.org/wiki/
    Polyamory_in_the_United_States

19 https://client.strategicbusinessinsights.com/vals/
    ustypes.shtml

20 Mike Maples Jr and Peter Ziebelman. *Pattern
    Breakers: Why Some Start-Ups Change the Future.*
    PublicAffairs, 2024.

21 https://en.wikipedia.org/wiki/
    List_of_countries_by_GDP_(nominal)

22 https://en.wikipedia.org/wiki/
    List_of_countries_by_GDP_(nominal)_per_capita

23 https://en.wikipedia.org/wiki/
    List_of_countries_by_total_fertility_rate

References

Mindset: The New Psychology of Success by Carol S. Dweck

Antifragile: Things That Gain from Disorder by Nassim Nicholas Taleb

Satisfaction: The Science of Finding True Fulfillment by Gregory Berns

Rethinking Humanity: Five Foundational Sector Disruptions, the Lifecycle of Civilizations, and the Coming Age of Freedom by Tony Seba and James Arbib

Range: Why Generalists Triumph in a Specialized World by David Epstein

Rocket Fuel: The One Essential Combination That Will Get You More of What You Want from Your Business by Gino Wickman

Supercommunicators: How to Unlock the Secret Language of Connection by Charles Duhigg

More than Two: Cultivating Nonmonogamous Relationships with Kindness and Integrity, 2nd Ed. by Eve Rickert and Andrea Zanin

UPLVL Communication: The Ultimate Solution to Save Relationships and Eliminate Hurtful, Damaging, & Meaningless Arguments by Kenya K. Stevens and Carl E. Stevens Jr.

"A generative vision model that trains with high data efficiency and breaks text-based CAPTCHAs" by Dileep George et al., https://www.science.org/doi/10.1126/science.aag2612.

A Thousand Brains: A New Theory of Intelligence by Jeff Hawkins

On Intelligence: How a New Understanding of the Brain Will Lead to the Creation of Truly Intelligent Machines by Jeff Hawkins

The WEIRDest People in the World: How the West Became Psychologically Peculiar and Particularly Prosperous by Joseph Henrich

Rabbit: The Autobiography of Ms. Pat by Patricia Williams

Myths of Innovation by Scott Berkun

Deep Utopia: Life and Meaning in a Solved World by Nick Bostrom

Pattern Breakers: Why Some Start-Ups Change the Future by Mike Maples Jr.

Kenya K Steves on Instagram: "I'm always so curious as to why we would continue to exist within and uphold systems that stifle our freedoms?" Instagram. (n.d.). https://www.instagram.com/reel/C_2z4wmRY8_/?utm_source=ig_embed&ig_rid=7c189d87-e54a-4976-a9ba-1f9d-193205f7&ig_mid=11A0E552-43F3-4C25-A06B-AC0314CD6369

Acknowledgments

This book wouldn't have blasted off without the fuel of some incredible people. Buckle up for a quick roll call:

My Crew: I would like to thank my beloved family. You were there through thick and thin. Thanks for being my mission control and keeping me grounded and humble.

The Engineers: I wouldn't have come up with my proposed solutions to our biggest challenges without the ideas of great thinkers and scientists. I've mentioned and quoted some throughout the book and bibliography. Thank you.

The Launch Pad: I'd like to acknowledge everyone at Igniting Souls Publishing, particularly my editor, Elizabeth Haller, who helped me clarify my thoughts and polish the ideas and presentation of this book. And also thanks to my social media agency WMG Communications.

You, the Reader: This book wouldn't exist without your curiosity. Thanks for picking it up and embarking on this journey with me. May it spark your imagination and propel you to DREAM BIG. Here's to reaching for the stars together!

This is just the beginning!

About the Author

Paul J. Ebreo is an author, entrepreneur, and polymath who fully embraces his highly varied skillset. He has a lifelong love of learning and teaching. With degrees in accounting and nuclear medicine, Paul has extensive formal experience in software engineering as well as both medical and technological fields.

Halo halo (pronounced hollow hollow) is the name of a cherished Filipino dessert, which was Paul's favorite childhood treat. It means "mix mix" and is a mashup of shaved ice, evaporated milk, sugar, flan, sweet red beans, shaved coconut, pinipig (or rice crispies), jack fruit, ube, and ice cream on top. These disparate ingredients and flavors become something extraordinary when they come together, and it is a perfect analogy for the convergence Paul seeks to create an amazing new world.

Paul sees his own life as a wonderful confluence of factors. As a Filipino, he possesses both Asian and Spanish heritage, but his surname is a Greek word meaning Hebrew. His native tongue, Tagalog, shares similarities with Malay. His friends and mentors have added to this geographical convergence, as they range from other Filipinos to African Americans, Puerto Ricans, Mexicans, Jewish Americans, Irish, Arab Americans, Germans, Polish, Caucasian Americans, Indians, and Greeks. These people and their diversity have instilled richness in his life from an early age.

Using his experience and talent to relate to anyone, he enjoys cultivating his "garden" of friendships. He believes in manifesting a vision of abundance, generosity, and kindness to all.

Connect with Paul at GoatWorldBook.com

CONNECT WITH PAUL

Follow him on your favorite
social media platforms today.

GoatWorldBook.com

THIS BOOK IS PROTECTED INTELLECTUAL PROPERTY

Instant IP [IP]

The author of this book values Intellectual Property. The book you just read is protected by Instant IP[IP], a proprietary process, which integrates blockchain technology giving Intellectual Property "Global Protection." By creating a "Time-Stamped" smart contract that can never be tampered with or changed, we establish "First Use" that tracks back to the author.

Instant IP [IP] functions much like a Pre-Patent since it provides an immutable "First Use" of the Intellectual Property. This is achieved through our proprietary process of leveraging blockchain technology and smart contracts. As a result, proving "First Use" is simple through a global and verifiable smart contract. By protecting intellectual property with blockchain technology and smart contracts, we establish a "First to File" event.

Protected by Instant IP [IP]

LEARN MORE AT INSTANTIP.TODAY